Judith Holder has a distinguished career in television, having produced some of the funniest people in the business, including Clive James, Billy Connelly, Dame Edna Everage, Victoria Wood and Lenny Henry. She produces and writes *Grumpy Old Women* for BBC2, along with other grumpy-related TV, and co-wrote with Jenny Eclair the hugely successful stage show *Grumpy Old Women Live*. She is also the author of the bestselling *The Secret Diary of a Grumpy Old Woman*. Judith lives in Northumberland and holidays as often as possible. Some people call that optimism.

By Judith Holder

GRUMPY OLD COUPLES
GRUMPY OLD HOLIDAYS
GRUMPY OLD WOMEN
IT'S (NOT) GRIM UP NORTH
THE SECRET DIARY OF A GRUMPY OLD WOMAN

Grumpy Old Holidays

JUDITH HOLDER

Illustrations by Noel Ford

PHOENIX

A PHOENIX PAPERBACK

First published in Great Britain in 2007
by Weidenfeld & Nicolson
This paperback edition published in 2008
by Phoenix,
an imprint of Orion Books Ltd,
Orion House, 5 Upper St Martin's Lane,
London WC2H 9EA

An Hachette Livre UK company

10 9 8 7 6 5 4 3 2 1

A CIP catalogue record for this book
is available from the British Library.

ISBN 978-0-7538-2380-4

Printed and bound in the UK by
CPI Mackays, Chatham ME5 8TD

The Orion Pu
are natural, r
made from w
and manufac
the environm

www.orionbo

Acknowledgements

Thanks to Benjamin Lee for his brilliant editing work on the material.

Thanks to Mike Parker, Ellen Parker, Rosie Dammers, and Will Chamberlain for their brilliant comedy input, and to the team at Liberty Bell – Claire Storey, Emma McKinney, Mark Duncan, Caroline Broome, Louise Mitchell, Simon Glass, Graham Smith and Stuart Prebble.

Also to our splendid grumpy celebrities:
John O'Farrell; Matthew Parris; Don Warrington; Stuart Maconie; Michael Winner; Nina Myskow; Jane Moore; Linda Robson; Jenny Eclair; Jenni Trent Hughes; Kathryn Flett; Rhona Cameron; Arabella Weir; Helen Lederer.

And finally, to Lucinda McNeile for her astonishing patience and attention to detail.

Information given in this book regarding travel is subject to user and author error, since the purpose of the book is essentially to make you realise how grumpy you are about holidays. The facts and figures have been plucked out of the ether for your amusement rather than your education – if you see what I mean.

Contents

Grumpy Old Holidays

1

Going Away

HOLIDAYS – WHO NEEDS THEM?

Normal people are at their happiest on holidays. But for grumpy people holidays can simply make them grumpier than ever, because the potential for disappointment is endless. You're thinking fabulous white sand beach, you're thinking coconut trees, you're thinking all-over suntans, you're thinking romantic suppers at sunset ... but get there and nothing's *right* (or even built yet), never mind *perfect*. And because holidays are designed to make you feel fantastic, because that's the point of them, they don't.

It's not like we all don't need a holiday. We so need a holiday. As a nation apparently we spend longer at our desks than any other nation in Europe; we work on average a 43.5-hour week, with one in six of us doing an appalling 60-hour working week. We even do an astonishing 36 million hours of unpaid overtime each year. So we certainly need holidays. The average UK worker takes between 21 and 25 days of holiday a year, 30 per cent of us take two or more holidays a year and we spend a staggering

£63 billion on them every year. We need a holiday really badly, and the more we need the holiday, the more potential there is for disappointment. Which is spiteful of holidays. They're like Christmas but with suitcases: you work hard all year to pay for them, look forward to them all year, and then you get there and the weather is unseasonably bad, the sun-lounger war is in full swing and the Russians have got all the best rooms. Why wouldn't we be grumpy?

Maybe holidays are also like Christmases in that you remember the good bits. You have one or two idyllic memories of a fun-filled holiday with someone you are madly in love with when your bikini still looked good on you or you still had a full head of hair, you remember that one lovely lunch when everyone in the family was getting on, the sun shone and the waiter brought the food quickly … and those good bits stay with you, and this means you carry on trying to recreate them. And so you take yet more holidays. You manage to delete from your memory the bad bits about holidays.

On the other hand – you could look on the bright side – a bad holiday is a great way of making you feel grateful to be back in your own bed and back at your own desk. Job done. As it were.

CHOOSING A HOLIDAY

Grumpiness notwithstanding, holidays are big business. Mini breaks, maxi breaks, adventure holidays, packages, off peak, on peak – you name it, we book it. And it's all got so complicated, like pretty much everything else in life. When my parents were my age and up till the early 1960s, you simply went for a fortnight to St Ives or Weston-super-Mare or Brighton or Blackpool, and you chose between a bed and breakfast, a campsite or a caravan. Even choosing when to go was easy. The factory closed down for a factory fortnight, which meant that everyone else in the

Midlands went on holiday at the same time, which must have made it conspicuously easy for burglars, and consequently Burnham-on-Sea or Canvey Island were chock-a-block with people just like you for the same fortnight. Which was good ... -ish. And it meant that choosing a holiday was a relative skip in the park. Then suddenly, in the 1960s, the package deal arrived. Suddenly you heard of people going to the Costa Brava or Brittany or Majorca, pronounced amazingly 'Mayorca'. Ordinary people no less went abroad – you didn't even have to be Alan Whicker or Cliff Michelmore. People came back with tales of bright uninterrrupted blue skies for a fortnight, cheap red wine, something called garlic and sea as warm as a bath. And all for about a third of the price of a week in Frinton-on-Sea. The rest, as they say, is history, and now there is so much choice on

> The average British holiday maker will travel 248,000 miles during their lifetime – the equivalent of going around the world ten times.

offer with holidays you don't know where to start. Now many of us take more than one holiday a year, we spend an obscene amount of money on trying to chill out from earning all the money to spend on the holidays in the first place – and so holidays are now properly important, properly significant and properly here to stay.

Choosing a holiday now is a dizzy but pointless array of options: winter sun, summer sun, long haul, short haul, mini break, maxi break. You could spend a solid fortnight browsing the Internet, comparing prices, flights and half- or full-board arrangements and still find that some other Smart Alec got their deal on Teletext, or at a bucket shop, or booked theirs at the last minute, or went standby and got it for a third of the price you did;

or they paid exactly the same price as you and the lucky so-and-sos got upgraded to a junior suite when you booked yours in January and are allocated the room that needs refurbishing next to the lifts or under the delivery area at the back of the kitchens where they reverse in and remove all the bottles at 2 a.m. And breathe … You could spend hours, days, browsing the net, scrutinising the brochure, looking at the photo of the self-catering versus the full package and still get there and discover they took the photo of the pool from a crane with the widest-angled lens imaginable, or took the photo of the nicest, poshest room in the complex while yours is so small you have to reverse into the room with your case as there is no room to turn around.

Travel-agent-speak is almost as bad as estate-agent-speak. Here are some useful definitions.

Travel-agent-speak

- Cosy = small
- Up and coming = building site
- Stone's throw from the beach = stone's throw from the beach (with a catapult)
- Buzzing nightlife = vomiting Brits until 5 a.m.
- Friendly locals = don't leave your drinks unattended
- Entertainment provided = someone who looks like Engelbert Humperdinck belting out 'Spanish Eyes' right under your balcony
- Bubbly holiday reps = holiday reps who are too hung-over to be able to answer any query whatsoever but who are on commission to flog you a boat trip for £50 a pop
- Unspoilt = looks like a war zone
- White-washed hill-top village = bring oxygen masks and crampons
- Picturesque = semi-demolished
- Hamlet = not even a shop

- Sun drenched = no shade at all anywhere
- Complex = think Butlins, think organised entertainment, think small children making a lot of noise
- All-you-can-eat buffet breakfast and dinner = bring elbow pads with sharpened corners for the Germans
- Close to the beach = a bus ride away
- Due to the proximity of the airport this hotel may be subject to some airport noise = hotel is on the end of the runway
- Transfer time two minutes = as above
- Popular choice for families = bring ear plugs
- Free kids = bring ear plugs
- Overflowing with character and charm = nothing specific we could say that was nice about resort without being taken to court
- Lively nightlife = don't expect to get to sleep before 5 a.m.
- Half-board available at a supplement = they have bouncers on the restaurant to check you're not sneaking stuff out
- Dinner is waiter served = they have had so much food walk out they are policing it
- Free courtesy bus to beach = the beach is an hour away
- Hotel may be subject to some traffic noise = people complained and took us to court last season
- Unhurried pace of life = service is unbelievably bad
- Flanked by cool mangrove swamps = next to sewage outlet
- Safety deposit boxes in all rooms = we get a lot of stuff nicked
- Sea rooms are available = to the Russians
- A full programme of entertainment = there is not going to be a minute's peace
- The apartments are pleasantly furnished = means it will look like a prison cell
- Video games = expect a lot of tattoos

Even something as apparently harmless as 'close to amenities' can have a sordid subtext.

> *I took my mother and very small daughter to Ibiza, and the brochure said 'suitable for families' and those words which I should always have been suspicious of, 'close to amenities', which actually meant it was on top of a shopping centre and it was the biggest toilet I have ever been to in my life. It was a tiny little flat and either side we had teenagers who played music all day long on their balconies; and the bar next to the swimming pool was playing some record which was, 'I'm talking to you bitch, I'm talking to you bitch'. It was absolutely hideous. The word Ibiza now just brings me out in a cold sweat.*
>
> Jane Moore

People are becoming increasingly adventurous about the destinations they visit on holiday, with 89 per cent of travellers going to a new country every time they leave the UK. France remains the most popular holiday destination for the Brits, with 83 per cent of people having visited the country, followed by Spain at 77 per cent. The USA is the third most-visited country for people in the UK, with Italy and Greece making up the rest of the top five.

WHO TO GO ON HOLIDAY WITH

Where to go is a significant decision when choosing a holiday, but who to go with is infinitely more significant. Go somewhere as dull as Bognor Regis with someone you are head-over-heels obsessively in love with and you are bound to have a good time – OK, you're likely to have a good time in bed, then. But go to the best hotel in the Caribbean with someone you dislike and inevitably you will come to loathe them, since you will be with them 24/7. Even at the Sandy Lane Hotel in Barbados you will more than likely have a truly horrible time. OK, that's overstating it, but holidays have a horrible habit of magnifying problems not solving them.

If you're married, then naturally choosing not to go with your partner, or choosing to go with someone else instead of your partner, or going with someone else's partner, will be interpreted as something of a snub. Likewise if you have kids, going without them, or going with someone else's kids, would be seen as churlish, impolite to the point of downright unacceptable; so you go with the family. And like it or not, the same frictions that exist at home will exist on holiday.

> *I am not a very good holiday person. I quite like to go on holiday but I can't find anyone to go with me. I've sort of narrowed down and narrowed down, and even my own family sort of flinch when I mention it now.*
>
> *Jenny Eclair*

When you're young, and particularly when you're single, who to go on holiday with is the main dilemma. It is a known fact that the moment you book to go on holiday with the current girlfriend or boyfriend or your new best friend, you will go off them instantly, on the way home from the travel agent's, and from then on, in the run-up to the holiday, the relationship will falter and shatter to such an extent that if it weren't for the holiday booked together in August you would have split up or decided not to bother to ever see one another again. That's a given – the curse of the holiday booking. You're heading for a tricky run-up to the holiday and a tricky-to-the-point-of-truly-terrible holiday, and you're going to have to hold it together until you get off the plane on your way home. It can get so bad that some people have been known to run away from the airport in their separate directions once the (already paid for) holiday is through. Because the other basic truth about holidays is that they put an enormous strain on any relationship. Again it's like Christmas – there is simply far too much opportunity for quality time together.

When you marry someone, the contract should say 'for better for worse, for holidays and not for holidays'. Either that or you could have a variation on the pre-nuptial agreement whereby you can opt out of holidays together, because chances are you will have tried a holiday out with prospective spouse before getting married (one hopes), so you know just how irritating their obsession with Roman ruins and castles are, just how annoying it is that they have to try to find red mullet on every menu, even in the Spanish equivalent to a Happy Eater, and just how irritating it is that they pack the sangria they are bringing home in your joint suitcase and ruin your white linen trousers on the way home.

Either that or you make sure your other half books the holiday, leaving you free to criticise, tut and generally moan to your heart's content because they got it wrong. Which is another way of deflecting the anger when your hotel turns out to be on a light industrial estate in Gdansk.

I'd much rather sort of push the old man to book it, because then, you see, if it all goes wrong it's his fault, and I do need somebody to blame.

Jenny Eclair

WHEN TO BOOK

Holiday goers divide into two categories: people who like things organised well in advance, and those who like to leave things to the last minute. Tragically people usually marry someone from the opposite category.

I'm an Internet holiday booker, I just type in the word 'desperate' and want to go away tomorrow night with three children at a time that's not in the middle of the night and up it comes it says, absolutely, that'll be £22,000, thank you very much.

Jane Moore

I find it really creepy when people know in January where they are going on holiday the following year in August. I think that's really quite sad. I think a holiday is something that on Saturday morning you decide, Hmm ... I want to go somewhere, and you get on the Internet and whatever comes up and the next day you've packed your bags and gone – that's a holiday to me.

Jenni Trent Hughes

One thing that is universally, utterly true is that going away on bank holidays is frankly stupid to idiotic. Bank holidays are for people who like queuing on the A38 and like being nose-to-tail on the M5 for hours on end with only a bun at a motorway service station to look forward to, or like a day at Gatwick airport navigating their way through the crowds of people who are flight refugees sitting on or draping themselves over some nasty plastic back chairs in terminal one.

In May 2006 2.1 million people travelled abroad for the May bank holiday weekend.

God is trying to get a message to us about bank holidays. When can you remember a good sunny dry August Bank Holiday? Or an Easter Monday nice enough to sit outside and have a picnic? It's God's way of telling us to stay at home at bank holidays.

BEFORE YOU LEAVE HOME

You book a holiday because you need some serious relaxation, but the list of things that have got to be done before you actually leave the house wears you out even more. Like organise the cunning burglar-deterrent timer light switches that go off and on to ward off potential opportunists. Burglars must cruise down the roads until they see a landing light on and bingo! – they *know* you're on holiday. Might as well leave them the front door key under the mat.

> *Well, the other reason it's difficult for me to go on holiday is that if you're going on holiday in Britain obviously you're packing your car, which means that all the local criminals can see that you're leaving your house for an extensive period, so that's my first paranoia setting in: I'm thinking, How do I pack the car little by little, or maybe I could siphon things off to someone else's house in small parcels and then pack from their house so that I won't be seen packing from my own house by the local crims?*
>
> Arabella Weir

According to the police and insurance companies we are not doing enough to prevent burglaries when we are away. Surveys have found that finding someone to look after your pets was a much bigger priority than moving valuables so that they could not be seen through the window, and a lot of us don't actually set our burglar alarm. This is the kind of checklist that is recommended

- Make sure your home looks as if someone is living in it. Closed curtains or blinds during the day may give the impression that no one is in (equally presumably open blinds or curtains at night might do the same).

- Use timer switches on lights and radios (aha – brilliant!).
- Fit mortice locks or bolts to all outside doors; fit strong locks to all downstairs or easily accessible windows.
- Cancel all milk and newspaper deliveries.
- Cut the lawn before you go away and trim back any plants that burglars could hide behind.
- Get a friend or neighbour to look after your home.
- Ensure all property is adequately marked.
- Do not put your home address on your luggage when you are travelling to your holiday destination.
- Lock the garage and shed with proper security locks, after putting all your tools safely away.
- If you have to have a ladder out, put it on its side and lock it to a secure fixture with a close shackle padlock or heavy-duty chain.
- Lock all outside doors and windows.
- If you have a burglar alarm, make sure it is set and that you have told the police who has the key.

Enough to put anyone off going away on holiday ... because doing that lot is going to take you a full week, minimum.

Then there's the pets to be taken to kennels or neighbours or catteries, wheelie bins to put out, plants to be watered, post to be taken in. Women with two children, a dog, a hamster, a catalogue habit and a full-time job wear themselves out doing all this before going on holiday – I know because I am one of them. We get a pre-holiday face, a ready-to-explode-into-rage-at-any moment-type face; we create a 2-metre exclusion zone around us of stressed-out, strung-out pre-holiday angst.

Keeping your pet in the picture

Leaving a cherished pet behind can be a real problem for adoring owners, but in a move likely they say to become standard in no time at all, one up-to-date kennel in Ireland has found a way to keep pets and their owners in touch even on holiday. The kennel has some special features, including heated flooring and soothing music, and it also provides a web-cam. Thanks to a series of web-cameras, the dogs can be monitored night or day. All their owners need to do is find an Internet café and log on to the kennel's website. While the 'pet-cam system' is only available for dogs at the moment, they hope to extend it to include all pets, including cats and birds in the future.

For those of us with teenage children who choose to stay at home to 'do revision', or for those of us who are scary enough to distrust the local helpful neighbour and set a trap for her, this kind of technological advance sounds very useful indeed.

PACKING

If you were wondering if there's truly much difference between men and women, packing for a holiday is proof positive that men are from Mars and women are busy packing a spare pair of pants. Women pack for weeks. The spare room becomes mission control; hundreds of clothes and everyday objects go missing because they go into the holding area in said mission control in case they are deemed essential for a fortnight in Majorca;

everything sits in neat piles, ready for last-minute inclusion or rejection. All sorts of things might appear in these sacred piles – everyday household objects like doormats, saucepans and toothpicks, as well as the more traditional wardrobeful of clothes. Everything has to be folded, cleaned and ironed in preparation for going into the case. For some reason when it comes to packing logic escapes women (I include myself in this, of course) – the fact that everything comes out of the case the other end like a crumpled, tangled, knotted heap is something which I choose to forget.

With packing, women assume worst-case scenario on all fronts, including weather fronts – in fact especially on weather fronts. Even when going to Greece in August women pack waterproofs, a jumper and it has to be said sometimes a woolly hat. Just in case. Because women are pessimists. What is a given truth is that if you only pack shorts, the weather will be unseasonably bad, and if you don't think you'll bother with the cagoule, you will spend your first two days kitting you and the family out in waterproofs. Because that's what holidays are like: uncooperative.

I've had enough very strange weather experiences on holiday to know that as soon as you pack the one bikini, the one pair of shorts and the espadrilles you will need a fleece.

Kathyrn Flett

Women are more than pessimists when it comes to holidays: they're catastrophisers – holidays bring out the hypochondriac in even the most relaxed woman. So normally women are busy in the run-up to a holiday packing up enough medical supplies for a field hospital. Paracetamol, Night Nurse, Day Nurse, mossie spray, wasp ease, plasters, splints, bandages, antiseptic wipes, anti-diarrhoea pills, the full monty – couldn't hurt to throw in a tracheotomy kit too. Women pack for all medical eventualities:

broken limbs, jungle fever, malaria – you name it, women pack for it. You just don't know what might happen ... And it's all logged in and ticked off with tragic attention to detail. Not that being a hypochondriac on holiday is a uniquely female attribute: some men, and even some very seasoned travellers, are self-confessed hypochondriacs – take the whole hospital with them.

> *Well, I take actually normally about 28 pills a day. I'm a great believer in pills. I take health pills, so I have to take my little packets of pills, and then I take various medications. I think it's important that if it's a Sunday or it's some time when you can't get anybody or you don't know anybody you have your basic survival kit, which is quite large in my case. But in Barbados there were these old Americans: they had a defibrillator with them. They were carrying around a big electrical defibrillator in case one of them had a heart attack, and they said to me, 'We've got a defibrillator, so if you've any problem you can use our defibrillator.' Unbelievable. I don't go that far.*
>
> Michael Winner

Then for women, there's the shoes and bags that go in the case. Men don't really get the shoes thing. They don't get the fact that you need a high pair and a low pair and a sensible pair and a brown pair and a pink pair. For men packing for a holiday is like life really – one for the beach and one for the rocky walk up to the ruin on the hill. Worse than that, men refuse to take packing seriously at all. They are in-denial packers – they just bung a few near-to-hand clothes into a bag. Result: the shorts-and-tartan-socks look, and it'll be no good asking them for some Savlon dry spray the other end.

> *I get the most room in the case, obviously – he doesn't want to take eight pairs of shoes – because that's the thing about*

holidays: you forget about how many pairs of shoes you need. You need the flat ones, you need the sandals, you need the high heels in case of something fancy, you need the ones that go with the other frock and then you need probably trainers in case you need to walk.

Nina Myskow

And it's no good trying to pack for someone else. There lies disaster, because you'll get to the hotel and find they've forgotten your flippers and snorkel and brought the wrong type of sunblock. Unthinkable.

The male approach to packing, however, as in low effort or no effort at all, is to be envied.

I envy male packing because it tends to start roughly about three hours before the flight for you to leave, and finishes sort of about two hours and 55 minutes before the flight's due to leave. And that's great. I mean I envy that. Mine starts about a week before, on average, I'd say.

Kathryn Flett

Women tend to be very organised about these things. They think ahead: they think I'm going to need this, I'm going to need that, I'm going to need the other. I just think, Well, if I haven't got it, I'll buy it when I'm there – you know, in the end if you're going somewhere warm, what do you need, more than a T-shirt, a pair of shorts and swimming trunks? That's all I need, really.

Don Warrington

I don't pack. There's never any point in packing. The earlier you start packing, the more anxiety it causes and the more you begin to worry about just how many pairs of underpants you need. The answer is two: one to wear and one to wash. The

best thing to do is leave it till the last 20 minutes before you have to leave the house and then just throw everything into a suitcase, and even then you usually take too much.

Matthew Parris

Not that everyone conforms to the gender divisions ...

> *I really overpack because I think what I'd never want to end up on holiday is like, Oh, I wish I'd brought – fill in the blank. So consequently the night before holiday I will be getting all 26 volumes of the* Grove Dictionary of Music *in my luggage, a colander, some brass-rubbing implements, a PlayStation 2. I just think, Well no, well you never know, no, I might need the collected works of D.H. Lawrence, you know, you never know, I might need a pith helmet ...*
>
> Stuart Maconie

The mistake we make, all of us, with packing is that we seem to assume that there are not shops in other parts of the world. So not only do we take all the clothes we could possibly need, even though we could buy them there, but we seem to think that you can't buy aspirins or Rennies or sun tan cream or a hair comb or sunglasses or anything anywhere else. Well, that's the male line on packing, anyway, but what men fail to understand is that yes of course women know that even in southern India there is shampoo to be bought or flip-flops to find, but women spend so much

---

IMPORTANT INFORMATION FOR THE HOLIDAY CATASTROPHISER

British tourists heading to Thailand face the highest risk of suffering traffic accidents, theft or food poisoning according to one survey. Researchers found that tourists in South Africa were most likely to suffer violent robberies or lose luggage in transit. Austria was the country where tourists were most likely to suffer a skiing or snowboarding accident (well, I suppose it would hardly be the Maldives). The Czech Republic topped the poll for pickpockets, while holiday makers in the Caribbean faced the biggest risk from insect bites and stings. The safest place to holiday was Ireland, followed by Belgium, Holland, Germany and France.

time shopping the rest of the year (especially in the run-up to a holiday) the last thing they want to do is go on holiday and have to shop. And anyway they might not have the right sort of shampoo.

While packing the case is obviously a female job, packing the car and closing the case is definitely male territory.

We divide the packing sort of down the middle in our family. My darling wife gets all the stuff out and lays it all out in the bedroom and I then have the job of putting it all in the suitcases and putting it in the car, so her job is about three days, 'cos that's making sure all the clothes are there, fit and are clean, and mine is like I make a big deal out of putting it in the case and closing it but, you know, that's a very responsible job.

John O'Farrell

If for reasons known only to yourselves you are going camping, or holidaying *en famille* in France for a fortnight, you are going to have to spend a good deal of time preparing and packing the car. For some reason you only ever prepare the car, pump up tyres or top up the oil when you are going on holiday, because naturally that's the only time you will ever blow a tyre or a gasket – going to Tesco you wouldn't.

There's the packing the car: now that really is a man's job, because only men can put that kind of intensity into positioning wellingtons, hampers, crabbing nets and all that. I couldn't care less about that – I'd be quite happy to just fill it all and then just empty it out at the other end, but my husband is quite keen on sort of controlled packing.

Arabella Weir

THE CAROUSEL

We can laugh at packing, we can envy last-minute packers, but get it wrong, do it carelessly and you can be the one whose case is coming down the carousel with your underwear spilling out all over the belt for all to see.

You think you don't care about what state your case is in, you think proper decent, smart luggage is a waste of money, until you see someone else's lovely matching gorgeous cases, and then yours looks rubbish and you feel a failure.

Well, packing is a very bad area for me in life. I almost, almost, feel very shaky when I pack. I feel quite hyper and anxious and, you know, the self-loathing begins because by this age in life I have failed to get matching luggage and when I go to the luggage belt and see the others' luggage I will get luggage envy.

Rhona Cameron

PACKING AS YOU GET OLDER

You'd think that as you get older you would get better at packing – better at knowing just exactly what you'll need for a five-day break or a city break or a fortnight in Greece. Well, you do actually, but sometimes, tragically, you find that you need more, not less: more very specific things from home are required for you to get in your relaxation zone, your comfort zone. You become a little bit distressed to be away from your own bed and your own comforts, and this, it has to be said, leads to some crazily eccentric and frankly old-boy and old-girl things going in the case.

People in their fifties also take a lot of breaks: nearly a third of people in this age group make at least three trips a year. They also tend to favour exotic destinations such as Malaysia, Thailand and Singapore.

That's a lot of slipper air miles.

We just spoil you with all this information, don't we?

No, the truth is holidays can be very disappointing indeed, and some of us would have quite a lot to choose from when asked which holiday would they say was their all-time worst holiday.

Do you want worst sunshine holiday? Do you want worst holiday in Britain? Do you want worst long-haul holiday? Worst close holiday, worst camping holiday, worst skiing holiday, worst hotel holiday, worst luxury holiday, worst honeymoon? I need something more to go on, really.

Kathryn Flett

2

Flying

I'm just about old enough to remember a time when flying was still rather glamorous, when Tressie Doll had an air hostess outfit which was all the rage, and we all coveted her blue-and-white BOAC shoulder flight bag; and some people – lucky people – actually had one for real, which meant you were rich enough to have flown the Atlantic. Then flying was something to boast about, and jet lag a must-have holiday souvenir. Now even for ordinary non-grumpy people flying can be challenging on the staying cheerful front. The glamour has well and truly gone. Unless you are flying first class, in which case I am afraid to have to tell you that glamour and luxury are alive and well, flying is now so not-glamorous it is verging on the inhumane. Flying long haul in economy is now so uncomfortable and cramped I imagine it is verging on contravening international human rights. Chickens in transit probably get more room.

Nevertheless, there are things about flying which still amuse me, like hearing the captain do his posh pushing-back-and-routing-over-eastern-Europe routine. I like silly bits of the safety demonstration, although I am gutted that now that no one can smoke we can no longer enjoy the immortal line 'Please extinguish all cigarettes before fitting your oxygen mask', which I always looked forward to. There are still the odd amusing moments, like hearing the cabin crew trying to pronounce the safety announcement in French or Spanish, or trying to pronounce Jean Paul Gaultier when they wheel the annoying duty-free trolley past, or trying to persuade us to be thrilled that the easyJet inflight magazine is 'ours to keep' – oh goody! These little things still amuse me. For about 40 seconds – and then, alas, there is sometimes still ten hours of flying to undergo before we get to our destination. Such is today's flying.

But flying – because there is still an upper class and a business class and a world-class traveller and premium economy and so many classes and prices that it makes you dizzy, since it is not a form of communism – still brings out the worst in people. People show off about their teeny weeny weeny bit of one-upmanship, such as their air miles, or their near miss over Narita airport in Tokyo, which is their way of telling you their company sends them in a slightly more expensive seat or sends them to Tokyo at all. It's all very tiresome.

SETTING OFF

Going anywhere by air for some reason always, always, always means starting out very early. I'm not sure why this is, since flying is the fastest form of transport, but this is always the way it works out. In the brochure the departure time looks quite civilised, but then you work backwards: one hour to get to the airport, add another half-hour for safety, two hours for check-in and hey presto, you're leaving in the middle of the night – just like last time. You're so worn out after working your socks off for 30 weeks solid, and you've had to clear your desk, finish the report at work, take the dog to the kennels, leave notes for the postman, and leave the back door key with the neighbours and be sociable to them (the latter being easily the most onerous), and you get to bed having finally closed your case and remembered that you forgot to remember your driving licence, and – here's the cherry on the cake – you set the alarm for 3.20 a.m. It feels as if you are leaving the house in the middle of the night. That's because it is the middle of the night. Which means, naturally, that you don't get to sleep until 2 a.m. because you are worried about not waking up for 3.20 a.m. and, despite the fact that you've set two alarms and your mobile to wake you, you think you are going to miss the flight. You finally get to sleep at about 3.18 a.m. and then all three alarm clocks go off, like clockwork. Which means that you get yourself into the car, and out of the house, with no breakfast, and at your age that is a nasty break in routine, a nasty way to start the day – which is a long-winded way of saying that you are in a very, very grumpy mood indeed. When you were a kid, going on holiday meant you were excited, almost as excited as you were on Christmas Eve when you knew Father Christmas was coming, or at least you pretended you did; you didn't notice getting up early – you were simply chuffed to be going on holiday. Now getting up at 3.20 a.m. is not exciting. It is very, very annoying indeed.

You get to the airport in the dark, and the first thing you have to do is find somewhere to park in a car park the size of Sunderland. Gatwick airport alone handled 32.5 million passengers in 2005 and the car parks can sometimes be full, which on the scale of anxiety rates pretty near the top to me; arriving to get a flight and finding you simply cannot find anywhere to park makes my palms go sweaty just at the thought. Next you wait for the courtesy bus. Then you give up waiting for the courtesy bus and wheel your wheelie along the car park the size of Greater Manchester to the terminal building. Then you wheel it to the right terminal building. Already that has taken 40 precious checking-in minutes.

Of course one person's idea of being late is another person's idea of being early. And it seems particularly cruel of God to plan things so that the punctual person is attracted to the non-punctual person, which is enough to get any holiday off to a bad start. In our house my husband likes to leave things very tight, everything timed to the last minute, and I loathe and detest rushing, so want plenty of slack. The compromise we reach is no good for either of us: he's dawdling, thinking we have all the time in the world, and I am on the edge of my seat in the taxi. Again, more grumpy faces.

Not that checking in and getting to the airport are any guarantee that in the end you won't actually be disastrously late, because some people take cutting things fine to extremes.

> *The people I can't understand are the people for whom desperate calls go out at the last minute. They've checked in but they haven't appeared at the departure gate. What are they doing? Buying an extra 14 duty-free teddy bears? Don't they know that the flight is going to leave?*
>
> *Matthew Parris*

OK, getting up early to get a flight is bad, but you could accept it, you could live with it a whole lot better, if it were actually necessary. But get to the airport and it soon becomes clear that everything – finding a parking space, finding a trolley, checking in, going through security – takes about 20 times longer than it would do if you could organise it yourself. And the cynical amongst us, and I am guessing that's us all, can only assume that they get you there so ridiculously early in order for you to shop, in order for you to spend more money, because they are not stupid: they know that you have more money in your wallet or more accurately your money belt than at any other time in the

HOW's your hurdling?

calendar year, and they get you there early in order to make you buy giant Toblerones, smoked salmon sides or cuckoo clocks. Get to the airport and things really start to make you grumpy. They're doing things specifically to make sure you're not in the holiday mood, sending you down silly zigzag queues to get to security when frankly a straight line would do, and then the other holiday makers start to irritate you big time for no reason other than they look as if they are in more of a holiday mood or nearer the front of the queue than you are.

You invariably choose the slowest check-in queue. Or that's the way it always feels, to grumpy people like me anyway. I stand seething and in a state of high anxiety about which queue

is moving the fastest, while my less grumpy husband, for
instance, just shrugs his shoulders. Maddening in itself. The
queue that seemed oh so much longer than yours overtakes you
while the person at the front of yours is still faffing on, trying to
check in their luggage to deepest Nigeria via Stockholm. Trouble
is all the best seats are going. In so far as there are any good seats.
Experience sadly tells me that even if you got to the check-in desk
the moment it opens the bulkhead seats or the ones with the
decent leg room have all gone, all reserved to people with very
efficient travel agents or people with more air miles than you.
Either way, by the time we get there we are lucky to be seated
together.

It amazes me that more people don't die in airports: some
check-in queues for long-haul flights are so long and so stressful
it's enough to bring on a heart attack. I'm talking about the
queues for economy, of course – obviously the first-class queues
are ostentatiously next to the economy ones, with a red carpet
and the most efficient staff on the books – they're not stupid, and
they create calm little microclimates of smiles, service and easy
relaxation. They could hide that bit at least. Sometimes checking
in can indeed take an hour or more – hence the apparently
absurd check-in times they put on your ticket. Old people, unfit
people, young children, grumpy people who are cheerfully challenged every day of the week find this hard. There are no seats
while you are waiting in line. In the heat of Los Angeles airport,
or Kuala Lumpur, these people are about to get on a flight for 13
hours in less space than a battery hen has. It is truly a wonder
people do not die while checking in of exhaustion, cardiac arrest
or sheer losing the will to live any more.

You eventually get to the check-in desk and wait for the heavy
interrogation designed to catch you off guard. I wouldn't like to
be an international terrorist trying to navigate my way through
these tricky unexpected questions.

My favourite is when they ask you, did you pack your own bag? Actually, no, I didn't, Manuel from down the street packed it. Did anybody give you anything to carry? Actually, yes, some strange man with dreadlocks came up to me outside the airport and he gave me this bag and asked me to carry it to his mother. You know, the questions are just absolutely inane, because if you were up to something you would say no and you know, if you were that stupid ... It's just silly, silly silly silly silly.

Jenni Trent Hughes

Who is going to say, 'Yes, I've packed lots of sharp things' or 'No, I didn't pack it myself and I don't know who did pack it and I don't know what they might have put in'? Obviously no one. We know what the questions are. All they need to say is, 'Are you aware of the security precautions and does this luggage comply with it?'

Matthew Parris

A 76-year-old New York man who joked about having hand grenades in his luggage was arrested on charges of terrorising. The passenger was checking in when he told the ticket agent that he had two hand grenades in his checked baggage, police said. The agent called the police, who searched the bag but found nothing. The man told the police the comment was intended to be funny. Police charged him with terrorising and he was taken to jail, missing his flight.

A pregnant woman was arrested at a Devon airport after causing a security alert. The incident happened when the woman joked to staff that she was carrying a bomb in her luggage. She was cautioned and later released, police said. The airport said it had a zero-tolerance policy in such matters.

A charter flight carrying more than 350 people made an unscheduled landing at Indianapolis international airport today after a passenger joked about having explosives, the authorities said. The passenger was charged with violating the false information act and making threats.

An American passenger told airport security he had a bomb in his luggage when they discovered a suspicious-looking object in his bag. In fact, the man was trying to disguise the fact that the black object was a component for a penis pump. He eventually told investigators he'd lied because his mother was standing near by and he didn't want her to know about it.

It's not even as if anyone can take a joke about it.

It's all frankly ludicrous. Stopping terrorists is a task so vast, so huge, so difficult that frankly in my view we should just put more effort into trying to get round the table and talk to them rather than devise even more stupid ways of catching us all out at the security scanner.

Airlines have, of course, wised up to this stress and anxiety as another way of getting money out of us, so pre-bookable seating is now big business and in the brochures you now find on offer the opportunity to guarantee your party will sit together on some routes. Pre-bookable seating is available at more cost and extra leg room seats are sold on some airlines in economy. No wonder the best seats are always gone.

Lots of things make us grumpy – that much is a given – but airports are particularly horrid places, universally chillingly similar, universally uncomfortable and wretched places where the idea is to kill some time and then kill some more.

It's not natural to be crammed in with so many people. In the Bible, isn't that supposed to be hell – people of all different languages kind of milling around aimlessly looking at those departure boards going click, click, click, click, cancelled, cancelled, cancelled, cancelled, cancelled ...?

Stuart Maconie

SHOPPING AT AIRPORTS

Finally you get through security and head for the departure lounge and now, as luck would have it, you have hours and hours of free time – more spare time than you've had all year. Trouble is the only thing to do is shop, and then shop some more. Thousands of special duty-free items are on offer that in normal circumstances you wouldn't dream of buying – but because there's nothing else to do, you find yourself stocking up on Scottish shortbread, Irish whiskey and disposable cameras.

More madness sets in. You buy yourself a lager for breakfast.

It's half past eight in the morning – would you do this at home? And the same applies in planes, doesn't it? You see those people eating massive plates of chips, drinking a stein of strong lager, half past four in the morning.

Stuart Maconie

I don't know if you've ever tried to spend an entire day at the Gatwick village, but as villages go its attractions are limited, you know. Once you've browsed round the Sock Shop and realised that none of those socks are particularly for you, there's not much else to do. And why do they call it a village? It's not a village.

John O'Farrell

Airports are basically shopping malls with planes spotted round the edge really. It's quite a bizarre concept. You go there, you shop like a nutcase for several hours, you get incredibly stressed, you shop more to de-stress yourself, and after your flight's delayed, what do you do? You shop a bit more. You eat some food you don't particularly want to eat and then you have to go and walk for about a thousand miles off on to one of those sort of pods at the end of a runway.

Kathryn Flett

Call me old-fashioned, but I thought the idea of a holiday is to get away from it all, but dream on because for now you're stuck in the departure lounge with thousand of new best friends. And some of them are going to be going to the same place as you, and you are going to be sitting so close to some of them on the plane that you might as well be snogging them. It's always at this point that you realise that the most annoying thing about holidays by far are other people, and unfortunately there are going to be an awful lot of them.

We always have this sort of family game where we sort of go right, OK, who do we least want to sit next to on the plane?

Jane Moore

And of course you can bet your bottom dollar that the person you would least like to be sitting next to on the plane is exactly who you are going to be sitting next to; worse, the family from hell that you've spotted during the jolly three-hour delay *will* be going to your hotel. And if you have come to the scary conclusion that the thing that makes you most grumpy, universally grumpy, unfailingly grumpy, is EVERYONE ELSE, then this is going to be very tricky indeed on holiday, because all of a sudden you can't just tut and huff at them in the street, as you are going to be holed up with them for a fortnight. And you thought family life was tricky.

All this speculation about which family from hell you are going to be subjected to for a fortnight is a game you will have plenty of time to play. Because gosh, imagine the surprise: the plane's delayed for an hour or five and you're in a miserable human pile-up with not enough chairs to go around. No choice but to zone them all out, play dead, drape yourself over a carpet in terminal three for an hour or two; and the icing on the cake is that your precious holiday time is ticking away.

It's a no-man's-land, a strange in-betweeny type of place, with no point to it at all except to make you spend money or try to forget how much money you have already spent on the flight/holiday/long weekend. Maybe the people buying lager at 6.30 a.m. are the ones who have got it right, so scoff you not.

Finally your flight is called, and there's a gate number and a flurry of excitement while you think, OK, it's all been a nightmare so far but the holiday is about to begin. You resolve afresh not to be so grumpy, not to be so fed up about it, and off you go. Gate 29 is obviously right at the end of a corridor a mile long, and it's like the start of a marathon: you are sprinting but pretending not to, as if getting the seat at the front of the gate is going to make any difference at all, but then one person starts to sprint so you all sprint.

Get to the gate and guess what? It's the size of a football pitch. Another holding area but without shops or Tie Racks. The field has narrowed; now you truly can see the people who you are going to be sitting next to, the people you are going to be in competition with if there are one or two free seats when the plane starts to taxi off and people make a run for them. More desperate attempts if it is a long-haul flight to get an upgrade – your brain tumour is playing up, your stepmother-in-law is in intensive care and you've just had a message to say she is now critical. Anything, you'll do anything to get away from the rabble that is the economy passengers. It's not that they are unpleasant in themselves but the miserable, wretched conditions you are about to be subjected to mean that they are willing to fight over every millimetre of space, every single freebie, every single thing which will make their flight more comfortable than everyone else's.

FINALLY GETTING ON THE PLANE

The woman at the counter gets out the silly microphone. You are under starter's orders, which explains why when easyJet do this they say, 'Please remain seated during this announcement,' presumably the result of one of the air staff being killed or maimed under the stampede once the passengers know the gate is open and they can board, because boarding first on easyJet means you have a choice of seats, and most importantly you have the first go at the overhead lockers, which means that the folding bike/double bunk bed/folding pram/convertible car you brought in as 'hand luggage' is going to take up masses of room and everyone else will have to sit with their bags, including their Tupperware and sandwiches, round their feet/on their lap. Again, the stakes are high.

It's not, it's truly not, that you can just sit back as a grumpee and think, silly buggers – what a stupid fuss about nothing. You are drawn into it. Everything counts now: which side of the steps you walk down, do you go on back or front steps or fan out and split up and see who gets there first and then bagsy for the rest of the party? Last on the bus might feel bad, but hey, you will be right by the doors when they open on the tarmac and first on the plane, so hang back and you might be better off. And this is all supposed to be a rest from the daily rat race!

You finally get on the plane and the scrum proper begins because now...

Well, if you are lucky enough to be on a flight with some spare seats – which is quite rare these days because they are combining flights the whole time, which is a nasty trick – there's that awful moment, you know, when you can see people, their eyes going, and they're staring and it is worse than towels and sunloungers, and you know that as soon as the seat belt sign is off they are going to be out there, but the thing is you're probably doing the same thing as well and you're thinking, Well, if you go that way, I'll go… It's, you know, it's just fraught, horrible.

Nina Myskow

Then there's the problem of where to put your hand luggage; you've crammed all your things into the regulation little holdall and everyone else has cheated and brought a wardrobe full. Then armrest war breaks out.

If there's a woman next to you her arm is firmly on the armrest. You dare not touch her arm because that would be molesting her. I do find that women like to surround themselves with a little buffer zone of personal space, so they put their belongings on a spare seat, if there's a spare seat next to you, and they put their arms on the armrests so that you can't put your arm there.

Matthew Parris

Needless to say, men think it's the women who hog the armrest, and women think that men do …

Men are the worst, actually, I have to say. They'll do this: they sit in their seat and there's two armrests, which means one each, but they use both. And why do men have to sit with their legs at this sort of angle? Why can't they just sit normally? They sit as if they've got a willy the size of, you know, Mount Etna or whatever.

Jane Moore

You thought that your fellow travellers were annoying in the airport, but now you are on the plane the potential for annoyingness is vastly greater. Their invasion of your (very small) personal space is maddening. And what's with the reclining seat thing? I mean, yes, if you are on an overnight flight from Dubai and you've all had your meal and they've turned the lights off and finished the movie, yes, OK then, recline your seat for an hour or two; but really 30 minutes in, or worse still just as they serve the meal, if the person in front of you reclines their seat you are in big trouble. All that can happen then is a Mexican-wave-type thing whereby everyone on the entire flight reclines their seat and no one gains a millimetre of extra space, but you're all in the same position as if you are having a filling at the dentist's. Great.

Then there's fat people to contend with on planes. Sorry, there is no better way of putting it. Some people on planes take up so very much more room than others, and we're not talking the amount of hand luggage they bring on.

> *The woman in the seat next door was so large that only a small section of her arse could get in the seats, so the rest of her was all mainly on my husband's lap but he – you'll be surprised to hear – is much more long suffering than me, cos I spend the whole flight going pah pah pah, as if, you know, my harrumphing was going to make her lose weight in nine hours.*
>
> *Arabella Weir*

> *When you get a flight and they measure your hand baggage, you have to put your bag in a special grid. People's bottoms should be put in that because there are people that get on flights whose arses would not fit into those, those grids.*
>
> *Jane Moore*

Fat people on aeroplanes are the bane of my life. I am a thin man; I am not overweight. I always end up next to an absolutely enormous obese person who spills all over me. Bits of them come over the armrest, bits of them invade underneath your feet, they can't confine themselves to one space, and I spend my entire flight crushed by this obese person who has paid the same air fare as me and that's what I object to. I know that fat people are saying that they want bigger seats. Fine, then they should pay bigger fares. I'll take a smaller seat and I'll pay a smaller fare, thank you.

Matthew Parris

Some of us feel so strongly about large people on planes that we just can't leave it alone.

One more on fat people: you're checking in your luggage, OK, and you are perhaps three pounds overweight, and the airline says to you, 'You have to pay four hundred and £97 excess baggage for this slight overweightness of your baggage.' You weigh nine stone. Behind you is someone who weighs eighteen stone, but they don't have excess baggage. Why should I pay for excess baggage when I'm nine stone less for the plane to carry than the person behind me?

Matthew Parris

A 29-stone man has spoken of his distress after space could not be found for him on a plane.

The poor man had to abandon his holiday after he could not fit into any of the seats. He said he had contacted operator Thomas Cook three times and was told there would not be a problem. It said seats had been allocated but the crew had realised extra space was needed and had acted for safety reasons and a full refund had been offered.

Passengers on a half-empty plane were shocked when an air hostess asked for eight 'fat' people to move. The eight passengers were asked to move to the front of the plane, as the captain was unhappy with weight distribution in the cabin.

Then the captain comes on all posh and county and you've been up for four hours already, and the best news ever is that despite the fact that you are belted in next to the family from hell, and you have as much personal space as Houdini, he says that air traffic control is reporting a very busy morning and that we have missed our slot, mainly because some toss pots from Liverpool got drunk in the bar before breakfast and had to be called four times and threatened with their luggage being chucked off. This is code for you are going to be delayed. Could be delayed by hours and hours, and if you are unlucky and you are sitting on the tarmac at Tunis airport or Istanbul you are going to be sitting in what is effectively an oven. Suddenly the delays and time you had at Gatwick airport where you could play dead and wander round Tie Rack for the fifteenth time seem, like, well, a holiday in comparison to where you are stuck now.

It's worse than a traffic jam on bank holiday Monday. Worse because at least then you can open a window. Next thing he'll come back on the intercom or whatever it's called half an hour later and distract you again with the route you'll be taking, should you ever be lucky enough to take off, and he'll tell you that you will be routing down over France, then the Spanish coast, and over Nantes and Perpignan, cruising at 30,000 feet. Like it makes a difference we know that. As usual it's all carefully worked out to distract us and make us think that something is happening when it so is not. The anxious amongst us are thinking the worst, looking out for fire engines coming alongside us or taking another look at their fellow passengers. Might they be hijackers? Are the drunks from Liverpool in fact religious extremists? Which is all another way of saying you just get a bit bored.

THE SAFETY DEMONSTRATION

Once the captain thinks there is a fighting chance of pushing back and moving off, the cabin crew can let rip with the safety demonstration. They can put the show on. The safety demonstration – it's hardly got much to do with safety, surely – is a little game we play, and it's a game of two halves. Either you pretend you're a jetsetter Mr Cool and haven't even noticed it – don't bother me with this now – or you sit up and nod supportively like teacher's pet so that if you're plummeting towards the sea you'll be the one picked out for the first jump on the slide, cross-referencing the safety card with their spiel, maybe asking one or two key questions by ringing the button – is this the sort of exit door you pull in or push out? Show you have been really listening. Except they probably won't know the answer anyway.

A parachute each you could understand – might be a sensible precaution; but little knots and belts and whistles – it's all a fairy story, a fantasy. Surely everyone can see that if we burst into flames or the wing falls off we're all going to forget where to tie our double bow and trample each other to death while hurtling to the bottom of the ocean. Now it's become a communal comfort blanket. The pointlessness of it all is beyond silly.

They spin it all out. Basically they tell you how to do a safety belt up and undo it, as if none of us has ever been in a car and had to do that before; where the exits are, as if there is going to be time to get out; and to switch our mobiles and any other electronic equipment off because it affects the satellite navigation. Well, that is a worry because be honest at least half of the passengers either aren't listening at all or don't want to listen, or are preoccupied with their laptop or don't understand the announcement anyway. It is left to bossy people like me to police it. And police it I sometimes do, which doesn't make me the most popular person on the plane, but hey, I don't care.

> The other thing about safety announcements is I would like to pick them up on one or two of the points. They say 'in the event of a plane landing on water' – well, you want to go, 'Sorry, just going back a bit there, landing on water, cos this is made of metal this plane, isn't it? So it doesn't sink, the metal doesn't sink, so how does that work exactly when we land on the water?' And they say, 'When in the event of water you've got a life jacket under your seat.' 'Oh, that's fine, I'm not worried at all. I can relax now, cos in the event of landing on water I've got a life jacket, so right, we just hop out, no problem, I'm reassured now.' How does that work, then?
>
> John O Farrell

One minute you are thinking how silly the whole safety farce is and the next you suddenly remember how jolly important it might – just might – be.

> I'm one of those people who glances, slightly patronisingly, at the cabin crew, who makes a bit of a show of ignoring it, which they really don't like, and then panics about ten minutes later because I think, fucking hell, it's a 737, it's not a 747 or it's an airbus not a jumbo. God, is the lifejacket under the seat or is it under the seat in front? And you have a moment where you think, My life might just be lost because I didn't actually pay attention to where my whistle is.
>
> Kathryn Flett

I assume that if there were any sort of crisis on the aeroplane I would be Mr Hopeless. They'd have to carry me off and give me a little raft of my own and serve drinks on it, you know, and tea, and sandwiches. Let's see if it happens – I'd like to know what the catering is on the life raft, quite honestly.

Michael Winner

I know you put it on over your head, but it's the tying up – why haven't they organised themselves into a proper tie thing that you don't have to tie with a bow? I did wonder, actually, thinking about it in a kind of doomy way, have they made it deliberately complex so that you will be distracted as the plane is plummeting, so you don't notice that you've fallen another 3,000 feet in two seconds because you're trying to do your bow up neatly? Could be.

Nina Myskow

Oh, I just love all of it – it's such a great story, isn't it? It builds nicely. The great bit about putting your life jacket on first before helping other people – that must be a dramatic moment. You know, you can imagine the strings swelling up at that moment – no Gladys, put yours on first before you help me, even though my arms are broken trying to rescue the pilot. I like the tying the little thing in a double bow, the bit with the electric light that will light up upon contact with water, topping up, taking your high-heeled shoes off before you go down the slide. I like it all; it's great. It's like a poem, isn't it, that everyone can recite, and sort of brings you out in a slightly cold sweat.

Stuart Maconie

CHILDREN ON PLANES

If you're unlucky enough to have to fly with a toddler on your lap, or worse still be sitting with someone else's toddler, the amount of room is beyond a joke – presumably they think we're all contortionists. You are stuck, wedged in, and if you weren't claustrophobic, you are now. You're bored, you've had it up to here, you're going to be staring at the back of someone's sick bag for a good 12 hours; with only the refreshing towel left to look forward to, you might try to sleep – *try* to.

> *Long-haul flight, waited on hand and foot, which of course never happens at home, watch a film uninterrupted – oh, bliss. And then of course I get on the flight and I've got the child behind me, kick kick kick kick. This happened to me once on a long haul. I'm going like, OK, the parent is going to say something in a minute to the child. No. So then I say, 'Would you mind? It's just that he's constantly kicking my seat.' She went, 'Well, he is a child and you know…' I said, 'Yes, I know, I've got children, but does he have to constantly kick the seat as he has been doing for the last two hours? Could he just maybe kick it by accident every so often rather than methodically and wilfully?*
>
> Jane Moore

> *Somebody told me a fabulous story. They were on a flight and there was this family and the kids were running up and down and screaming and the parents were doing nothing, so the stewardess looked around and called the child over and said, 'Here's the deal: if you don't stop running up and down I'm going to make you go play outside.' Brilliant. Worked a treat.*
>
> Jenni Trent Hughes

I had an incident travelling recently where I asked a man if he wouldn't mind not tickling his child because it was causing hysteria, and me and the other passengers to have a, you know, an uncomfortable journey listening to the child screeching, to which he turned round and said, 'It's a two-year-old – what do you expect? It can either laugh or cry, your choice.' And I said, 'Well, with your child's extreme personality, perhaps you'd like to not tickle it – it might help.' I think people without children should all have business class and, oh, children in business class, no, no, no, no, no. No, no, no. I want there to be a childless class.

Rhona Cameron

I do have an idea which could catch on: ejector seats for passengers who are annoying. They have them in the RAF, don't they? Sod the complimentary wash bag and slippers – this would be good fun.

NOVELTY FLIGHTS

One travel company organises clothing-optional holidays and is to run what it claims is the world's first nude flight.

It has chartered a Boeing 727 for up to 170 passengers. The crew will be professionally dressed, and passengers must be fully clothed for check-in and take-off.

Only when the plane has reached its cruising altitude can the passengers strip off.

A German man is suing an airline after being kicked off a flight for being too smelly.

He had spent the day sightseeing in the hot Hawaiian sunshine, was asked to leave the plane in Honolulu when the person sitting next to him complained.

AIR QUALITY ON PLANES

Just when you thought you were as grumpy as you could get about flying, I'm about to make you even grumpier. Because the lack of leg room is one thing, but the air quality on board is something else. The further back you get, allegedly the worse it is – so much so that some sources say pilots get ten times more oxygen than the passengers get at the back, and that is the most hideous example of first-class one-upmanship so far. Apparently one way of filtering out the germs is to wear a mask, or if you don't have one with you wear a bra over your mouth (padded, ideally), which is one way of clearing a bit of personal space around yourself I guess. The air quality on a plane is ideal for bacteria to multiply, apparently, it being so dry and also not circulating. We are all jammed in closer together than we are in schools or trains, and look how low the ceiling is. It gets worse and worse. In-flight dehydration is something else to worry about, but whatever you do don't ask for a glass of water from the plane. Drink bottled only, and you are supposed to drink at least eight ounces of water every hour en route and then spray your face with water on the hour. Won't you be the popular one! Another tip is apparently to apply an edible vegetable oil inside your nostrils to protect the delicate membranes from the dry cabin air. Organic olive oil is the best. Again, watch those fellow passengers ask to move seats … Job done indeed.

NERVOUS FLIERS

Most grumpy people have clocked up an astonishing number of air miles, but even we experienced are still a little nervous of flying, especially, it has to be said, grumpy old women –- we catastrophise, we get on a plane and assume the worst. We don't like turbulence, we don't like it rocking about, we don't like it

ONE WAY TO KILL TIME DURING THE FLIGHT

Those in Atlanta seeking to join the 'Mile High Club' by having sex in an airborne aircraft can now do it for $300.

The Mile High Atlanta service has now gone up 75 times.

Couples get a custom-fit bed, brand new sheets and a complimentary bottle of champagne, and the pilot pulls privacy curtains and dons headphones as a courtesy. He also provides couples with a kitchen timer to keep track of their hour and avoid being interrupted.

turning corners, we certainly don't like take-off. Then again we don't like landing either. Which makes us grumpy with knobs on in the air.

If you are prone to worrying, then flying is fraught with worrying possibilities. And of course if the plane starts to wobble about, then worry sets in big time.

I don't like the tremoring. I don't mind if we go up nice and smooth, and I quite like being able to see. I like seeing green land because green land means field. What I don't like is when we get above that bit and we go through the cloud and that's where you get a bit of cloud turbulence and, you know, they say to you it's like driving down a bumpy road, but there's something about it that makes me very nervous – turn into a woman that's seen a mouse in the corner. So I do sometimes have to resort to medication.

Jenny Eclair

Best not move around, not jiggle the plane about too much.

I don't like going to the toilet either because I think that if people walk up and down the aisle you can tilt the plane. I just want everyone to sit still basically, preferably with their hands on their head, just sit still like that.

Jenny Eclair

The worriers – it seems – worry for everyone.

There is a term for people like me who are hypervigilant, so when anything goes boooo, you go, what's that, what was that, is that the wing coming off? As if they'll have a noise, you know, to alert the pilot that the wing's come off – oh, I see the wing's come off. What's that? It's just a Dutch business-man ordering another schnapps, isn't it? That's all it is, but I think, Oh you know what that will be, that's a code – it's like in theatres when they ask for Mr Sand, it's a code: we're crashing.

Stuart Maconie

AIR CABIN CREW

Back in the golden age of air travel, flying was really something – not that any of us plebs got a look in. You had to be properly rich and famous to fly anywhere, pampered by glamorous host-esses serving all you could eat caviar.

Now, yes, everyone can afford to fly, but you'll be lucky if the hostess throws you a packet of pretzels. Suddenly the gist of it is sit there, sit down and shut up.

I don't believe in having air hostesses that are under 40, I real-ly don't. You want matrons, you want sort of slightly fat women who are going to tell you not to be so silly.

Jenny Eclair

Naturally with all this glamour and excitement men decided to get in on the act, so now we have male as well as female trolley dollies, but you can't please everyone.

It has to be said that cabin crew find passengers rather annoying, and in a secret poll this is what they said they find the most annoying about passengers:

1. Passengers asking you what land masses, mountains, patches of green rivers, etc. are throughout the flight and expect you to know.
2. Passengers travelling on charter flights back from sunny Spain etc. to rainy cold UK in shorts and a T-shirt and complaining about the cold when they land.
3. Passengers with special dietary needs who (apparently) on seeing the veggie/kosher special meals suddenly do not eat meat and want you to prepare a special meal for them. Also some vegetarians see what vegetarian choice is available and suddenly remember they do eat some meat, and fish is not really meat, is it?
4. Those passengers who desperately need wheelchairs for embarking on an aircraft but can suddenly walk on arrival.
5. Passengers sneaking into the crew rest bunk bed for sleep.
6. Mothers with babies not bringing any nappies or food on long flights and expecting the crew to have everything for them.
7. People who leave their teeth, glasses or pens on the meal tray and expect you to pick through 300 meal trays and rubbish to find them.
8. Celebrities who eat nothing all flight or who binge on chocolate and then disappear to the toilets to throw up.
9. Celebrities who refuse to talk to crew when ordering their meal and all communication is done via their assistant.
10. Passengers who buy one business-class ticket and then expect the rest of the family to be upgraded if there are spare seats.

11. People who cross through the curtain when lights go down and think they won't be discovered.
12. Passengers travelling from dry countries who take the opportunity to get plastered on alcohol.
13. Arguments over the empty row of seats once everyone has been seated. It's war.

You hear a lot of people complaining that male cabin crew are all gay these days. Well, I have a complaint and that is that there are still some straight airline stewards. What are they doing as airline stewards? They are absolutely in the wrong job. You want to make a slightly loaded remark, a little bit of innuendo, and you assume that the airline steward is gay and will understand. Suddenly this straight 'Who are you looking at me jimmy' sort of fella looks back at you.

Matthew Parris

I suppose flying is cramped and uncomfortable for passengers, and so it's pretty much the same for the crew too; and the more grumpy we all get and the more miserable we become, the worse their jobs are.

FOOD ON PLANES

Eventually, if you're lucky, the food arrives – well, something arrives. Food on planes is bad to the point of not really resembling food as we ordinarily know it. I can't think of a worse example of the gulf between what they describe it as and what arrives on your maddeningly small flap table thing – especially on long-haul flights, when they are desperate to distract you by any means possible that doesn't involve much money, so they give you a menu, with descriptions designed to trick you into thinking that what is going to arrive will be like something you might order in a restaurant. You spend a happy minute and a half deciding whether to plump for the boeuf bourgignon or the salmon en croûte, only to find that even if they do still have a choice left what you get is exactly the same as every tray of food you have ever got on any flight ever, which is a dollop of white substance which is supposed to be mashed potato but has not seen anything that ever resembled a potato at all, and some gluey dark stuff with some carrot cubes in, and yes, you've guessed, a bread roll, a piece of cheese and a pudding with shaving cream on it. The best you can say is that it will alleviate the boredom for about two minutes. Then guess what: the person in front of you decides to recline their seat into your face, literally.

> *You think, I can't eat this swill but the thing is you eat the lot, you eat everything, you eat absolutely everything, and I look across at other people who have failed to eat and I think, what is wrong with them, gosh how restrained they are, and I'm made to feel guilty because I've eaten a lot, but what else can you do?*
>
> *Nina Myskow*

The breakfast is even more dismal. Be unlucky enough to be on an overnight flight and you might wake to find a tray of yellow stuff which is basically the mashed potato but painted yellow, a cocktail sausage and a piece of meat that looks and usually tastes (I imagine) like a dog chew. Enough to put you off cooked breakfasts for ever more, which of course might not be a bad thing in itself but not what you need after ten hours sitting in the most uncomfortable chair you can remember. Even being seated next to someone else eating it can be challenging, particularly in turbulence.

MISERY OF LONG HAUL IN ECONOMY

You're in a space the size of a bedsit fridge, you're hemmed in, you haven't even got room to get down to your bag on the floor ... You've eaten your 'food' within two seconds, look at your watch and you have a mere eight and a half hours left to kill. Such are the joys of long haul in economy. It'll take more than 32 channels of easy listening and a lousy film to take your mind off it. Even watching the film is problem atic.

All you want is for time to pass; all you want is to get there, to knock yourself out somehow. Anything to zone yourself out of the crampy, smelly, hole you are in. And face it, it's not like you can think, I've had enough – sod it, I'm getting off.

I think since planes have become so miserable, unless you are at the front end, the pointy end, down the back they are a living hell. I think the maximum cut-off point for a flight before you lose your mind, in economy, is probably about four, four and a half hours. So you can get to the outer reaches of the Greek islands from Britain before things start to get really, really tough.

Kathryn Flett

Overnight flights are unanimously the worst. There's only one thing worse than not being able to sleep on an overnight flight.

There is nothing worse when you cannot sleep than seeing other people sleeping, you know, sleeping like babies. I mean, you want to go and get really close to them and say wake up, just because you can't do it yourself. It is really annoying, it is terrible.

Nina Myskow

Overnight flights are – as you might expect – the worst because your inevitable inability to sleep, and the fact that the cabin crew are told to turn all the lights off while they have a nice rest, means the boredom will reach panic level. Worse still, the loos have to be braved.

> *They are very small, the cubicles, and you move your elbow and you do the flush and it sucks your womb out, you know.*
>
> *Jenny Eclair*

Worse even than going *to* the loo on a long-haul flight is sitting *near* the loo.

> *That actual back seat, I tell people, please avoid this if you really want to do yourself a favour, particularly if you are on*

When cabin fever turns to air rage

Some surveys have found that air travellers are more likely to suffer from stress and anxiety or find themselves displaying 'air rage' than experience dehydration, extreme fatigue or nausea, according to a survey on in-flight health problems.

Ear pain is the top complaint, followed by swollen ankles or feet and aching muscles and joints.

Stress, anxiety or 'air rage' was the fourth most common complaint, with many respondents surveyed saying they had experienced these feelings while in the air.

Figures have shown a large increase in the incidence of disruptive passenger behaviour on board UK flights compared to the previous year. A government body warns that the increase may be to do with better reporting methods rather than an increase in actual incidents. (Yes, right...)

long haul and it is an overnight flight, because I've sat in the back row and it is by where people queue for the loos and it is also by the bulkhead where the little porthole window is, so people always are queuing for the loo and then they think they will look out of the window so they lean forward and of course they are waiting for the loo so they lean forward and fart. So you wake up in the middle of the night and you think, Oh God, what is that? 12 hours of that between Singapore and Heathrow is not worth anybody's money.

Nina Myskow

No wonder when they open the doors on arrival after a long-haul flight the stench is apparently shocking. Oh the joys of modern air travel…

THE CLASS SYSTEM

The class system is alive and well in the sky.

Some of us, if we're really, really lucky or really, really famous or we grovel till it's embarrassing, might get bumped up to the posh end, might get upgraded. And unless you have been up the posh end and witnessed it at first hand you don't really get why people will try anything, and I mean anything, to get themselves bumped up. How different can it be? Totally different is the answer. In fact it looks remarkably like being in intensive care but without being ill.

You do see people being absolutely shameless, walking and saying can I have an upgrade? Well, I love that sense of entitlement. I love that idea that you would think that some-body might say yes. I can go through that sort of scenario in my head and I just know they're going to say no, why?

Kathryn Flett

And they will flaunt it, making you look, swishing silly curtains to and fro, making you walk past seats the size of double beds on your way to the cattle truck – all designed to make you want it.

Upgrades are frankly too good for the kids.

A famous TV presenter and his wife were in business class and they put their children in economy and I think, makes perfect sense to me, absolute, perfect. Why, why do kids get to travel? You know, they are not earning money, they're smaller, they should be happy they've got a holiday, and if Mum and Dad have earned all the money and want to sit in business class – so be it..

Jane Moore

I accidentally ended up in business class and it was on an aeroplane where the business class seats face each other and they are doing the safety announcement and you know how they always tell you brace position – you know, hand over your head, lean forward – and then they said, 'But if you are sitting in the reverse seats just fold your hands over your chest and lean back', and I thought, God, these suckers even die differently than we do.

Jenni Trent Hughes

This class structure, it seems to me, has to be stopped. A revolution, a people's revolution is what is required, and in the interests of that revolution I feel the need to share with you how nice it is up that posh end.

The best way to fly is in one of those big jumbo jets where you walk in and there's a staircase. I like a staircase in a plane. I like to go to the top deck, you get a better view, and so I did once do a flight to Australia. I got in, you turn, you know, whichever direction it is that's posh, up the stairs and then you're in this first-class lounge thing and it's like you're in an armchair. That's the difference, really, I think. When you crash in first class it's like crashing in a nice comfortable armchair, whereas if you crash in standard you're crashing in a deck chair and it's really going to hurt your face.

Jenny Eclair

It's so different that it's shocking that in x amount of feet of tin, hurtling bizarrely through the sky, there can be abject misery down the back end and a blissful world of relaxation and pampering massages and banter with helpful staff and really quite nice food and champagne on tap and you can't believe that these are in the same space, the same physical space.

Kathryn Flett

To add insult to injury they pull a little curtain closed so that the people in economy class can't actually see the others living it up in first class and business class. I make a point of pushing the curtain back again whenever I can.

Matthew Parris

It wasn't until I got upgraded myself that I realised that when you land they let everyone off the pointy posh bit first, and make everyone in economy behind the sacred curtain wait until the first-class lot have taken every scrap of their belongings and their freebies (considerable) before anyone in economy is allowed off. I just thought it was taking everyone a long time to get off, but no, they are all held back, as the riff-raff were in the movie *Titanic* – spookily and scarily rubbing in the fact that if you are in economy you are worthless scum, and if you are in first class you are worshipped as gods. It's called capitalism.

But let me tell you, if you are amongst those first-class people, you would boot anybody who dared to come out of cattle who wanted to get out before you. You'd definitely want to do it first. It's awful, isn't it?

Nina Myskow

Well, first class is the way to sleep, business class is a way to sleep roughly and economy is just – you just have to drink or take diazepam.

Rhona Cameron

Go one better still and hire your own jet. They're probably called easy private jets.

The biggest mistake I ever made in my life was not to take private jets earlier, cos airports are horrific. You start a holiday usually at an airport, and that is hell on earth: they lie to you, they say the plane's leaving in 20 minutes, the plane is not leaving in 20 minutes, you're lied to, you're shovelled about, you're cattle – ghastly.

Michael Winner

Great idea. Until you realise the cost. It makes first-class fare on a normal plane seem like a rock-bottom bargain.

Your private jet hire is very negotiable, actually, but I would say a normal return to Nice going on one day, coming back a day later, would be between £18,000 and £20,000. That's why I never take people who say we'll pay half the fare and we'll come. I say no, I don't want you to pay half the fare, I'm paying full money to get away from people like you. I don't want people on the plane with me, people who may be late, people who bring extra baggage. With a private jet you go, I go, mainly to Northolt, which is an RAF airfield. There's a tiny

little lobby, you walk straight through to the plane and it takes
off like a taxi.

Michael Winner

JET LAG

Get there after 12 hours of living hell, and chances are the jet lag
will kick in. And to think you signed up for all of this of your own
free will. What were you thinking of?

What I do have trouble with is stomach lag, cos my stomach just
sort of never seems to catch up, you know, so I wake up at seven
o'clock in the morning and I want chicken, you know, and about
ten o'clock at night, OK, time for scrambled eggs now. I am
awake, I am compos mentis, but the stomach takes a couple of
days to catch up with what's going on.

Jenni Trent Hughes

I wonder about jet leg, I sometimes wonder if it's something
that's simply promoted to explain people's bad performance at
business conferences, or indeed something that explains away
why we all arrive at our destinations feeling so completely rubbish but doesn't incriminate the airlines. Because unless you have
been flying at the pointy end, chances are you are indeed going
to arrive feeling that you need a holiday so much more than you
did when you set off.

Think your flight was bad ...

A flight was found to be infested with over 1,000 mice. The
plane was covered with nests and faeces and whenever they
got hungry they would chew through insulation and wires.

A pilot had to fend off a four-and-a-half-foot black snake
while maintaining control of the single-engine plane with one
hand.

Top five written complaints about flying

Delay: 19 per cent
Mishandled baggage: 15 per cent
Flight cancellations: 9 per cent
Reservations: 8 per cent
Overbooking: 7 per cent

Worst films to watch before getting on a plane

Alive
Final Destination
United 93
Airport
Air Force One

3
Hotels

You've had the journey from hell. It's taken you eight hours and you had anticipated it taking you three, the transfer bus was the last to leave the airport (idiot fellow holiday makers went straight to the bar on arrival), your hotel was the last on the drop-off, the transfer journey was supposed to take 40 minutes but for some reason, they said because of local flooding and land slides, your transfer journey took two hours, hugged the side of a mountain on a dirt track road, and when the driver wasn't smoking he was on his mobile. And you are tired, hungry and fed up. It hasn't been exactly relaxing so far. Nonetheless, while you sit in the coach dropping off all the other holiday makers, their hotels look reasonable, some look pretty good, and you hold on to the foolish notion that your hotel, when it eventually comes, will be as nice, if not nicer …

The rep is in full swing, being chirpy chops, making out the place is Mustique when in fact when you look out of the window it looks more like a war zone. She's stating the obvious, like the fact that you are on the road from the airport, or telling you about the currency. Other people on the coach show off that they got their holidays last minute and paid a tiny fraction of what you did when you booked yours in January, so face it: the odds are stacked against you having a good time. Nonetheless, while you have not arrived at the hotel you can still tell yourself – and you do – that the journey from hell and all the preparation so far to get you to this point, including all the money, have been worthwhile; your hotel is going to be secluded, quaint, full of local charm and have a view over the sea to die for, and you are going to have a fortnight of chilled relaxation.

You get to the hotel and check in, and you can remain optimistic no longer. OK, your hotel does not have a coin-operated washing machine in the lobby, but it has an Alsatian on a chain, and reception is a riot of formica-and-teak effect. It's more *Crossroads* motel than Four Seasons. The only plus is at least it's actually built.

Sadly this is the story of my life. I once went to Barbados for a fortnight, and of course naturally now you are feeling a little bit envious of me, except that if I tell you that we were at the bottom of the food chain, hotel-wise, you will understand. The best way to explain it is in descending celebrity visitor order. Pavarotti was at Sandy Lane (along, I presume, with Michael Winner), Rik Mayal was at the Colony Club, Frank Bruno was at the Almond Bay and the hotel we were in was so dreadful I have deleted the name from my memory, but the 'celebrities' in our hotel were the under-16 Swansea netball team. Got the picture? In fact I know where all those real celebrities were staying because our hotel was so depressing (and depressingly inland) and the pool so dirty that we played the I'm-staying-at-a-more-expensive-hotel game, and we got quite brazen about it, marching in to the Colony Club or Almond Bay and plonking ourselves on one of the sun-loungers and ordering drinks, as if we'd just popped down from the room for a lollabout. Worked a treat. But the crucial thing, if you are going to play this game, and I would highly rec-ommend it, is to discover where they give out the hotel beach towels, since otherwise the legitimate guests are all going to be lying on blue-striped or yellow-striped or bright apricot ones, and your Winnie-the-Pooh or England one is going to look very out of place and scream out intruder; but once you've blagged a towel or two out of them you're in business – just rinse it through every night and you're well away. Get cheeky with it and swap it for a clean one next day. They just think you're staying in the hotel. But don't try bringing the under-16 Swansea netball team with you, that's all.

CHECKING IN

The first anxiety is which room you are going to get. The lobby might be hideously downmarket, the resort your idea of hell, but if the room is looking out to sea or is a sumptuous junior suite, things can still be OK: the holiday can be salvaged. Clever, nerv-ous, grumpy people know that whatever it says in the brochure, whatever the rep tells you, some rooms are nicer than others – correction: some rooms are a great deal nicer than others – and once you know where the good rooms are, once you know where the refurbished wing is or the wing overlooking the bay, you so do not want to get into the room with the eighties ruche curtains, or the one that has seen so many smokers the whole thing reeks of Benson and Hedges and the eiderdown has seen a lot of rumpy-pumpy action. On a really bad holiday you can get a room where you don't really feel like taking your shoes off, never mind getting into bed.

It has to be said that women have more of a nose for what kind of better room might be on offer up the corridor than the men. My husband can be bounding about with some enthusiasm on arrival in the room, marvelling at how nice the TV is or how roomy the wardrobe, and I'm off down the corridor finding out the numbers of the room I want to change to.

Part of the trick is to get off the coach first, sprint to reception to check in, cop a load of your room and start complaining before anyone else gets the chance to change theirs, leaving nothing to chance. The other is to go to a hotel where the Germans or the Russians are not in residence, because for some reason German travel agents and Russian travel marks on the door where someone has tried to get in – none of these is a good sign. Agents get the best rooms. You get the one overlooking the shopping mall or the air conditioning vent and they get the ocean view or the pool. It'll all be down to money, of course, in the end, or the strength of the pound or the mark or whatever. Or just as likely that the Germans and Russians are very, very scary when complaining – probably more scary than any other nation. We should watch and learn.

There are some tell-tale signs of a bad room or a bad hotel. For example, shampoo in dispensers is a bad sign, and anything with the word 'quality' in the name is a bad sign. Horrid to really nasty prints on the walls, some sledgehammer marks on the door where someone has tried to get in – none of these is a good sign.

I mean, hotels, you know, they never, ever, ever, ever look like they do in the brochure, possibly because they're not actually the ones in the brochure – that quite often happens. Or they're shot from an angle, and of course digital photography now, you know, means that you can do anything really.

Kathryn Flett

Even in a posh hotel you can get a stain on the carpet and there's no way back from a stain on the carpet, some greasy, something nasty and you think, Oh, God, what was that? You know, that's always dreadful. A pubic hair anywhere, you know, just in an unexpected place, that, and you just – I don't know whether you change rooms or whether you just pretend it wasn't there or, it's just awful.

Nina Myskow

Some of us take changing rooms very seriously indeed.

It's quite normal for me to move rooms several times in a hotel, but it's also normal for me on the same evening to move hotels and to have two hotels that I'm not sure about. I will often keep the room on hold at one, get a taxi to the other, have to go in, sit down, practise positions, sitting on a chair, the window, lying down, see, and then go back to the other hotel, and the whole evening perhaps is wasted in moving from hotel to hotel, and when people get to know me they dread it.

Rhona Cameron

Whenever I travel, I travel with four extra sarongs and a vase and before security I used to carry a screwdriver as well. What for, you might ask. If I go into the room and I don't like the décor, I have to completely redo it. Paintings on the wall that I don't like, they come off – they go under the bed. I don't like the bedspread – some sort of, like, you know, manky polyester thing – gets folded up, put in the back of the closet – and sarongs everywhere.

Jenni Trent Hughes

COAT HANGERS

What is it with hotels and coat hangers? They're cheap enough, for goodness sake, and yet they nail them to the rack with those stupid ones that don't come off, or simply don't give you enough of them. Either way, you can bank on having a fisty fight with them for a good twenty minutes as you try to get your clothes hung up in the wardrobe.

Coat hangers in hotels are one of my big bugbears because I hate those ones that you can't get off the thing. A seasoned international traveller such as myself knows – I've learned from James Bond – a great trick when your shirts get all creased up in your luggage: hang them in the shower, and I'm passing this on – this has now gone like trade secrets, hasn't it? Hang them in the shower for 20 minutes, very hot. All the creases fall out, but you can't do that if you can't get the bloody coat hanger out of the – and another thing that annoys me is, you pay 200 quid for a hotel room, and I think, I'm all right for coat hangers, Mr Rocco Forte, you know what I mean? I won't nick your coat hangers, honestly.

Stuart Maconie

There are two kinds of duff coat hanger situations. One is when you open the wardrobe and there's all this motley crew, like a Marks and Spencer's one, a wire one, different ones all kind of jumbled together, they all kind of clang and mate and you can never get them apart. And the other kinds of coat hanger which I think I hate even more are those ones that are actually attached to the rail so you're having to get into the wardrobe to hang things up and then they clang against each other and you can't get them off … Can somebody invent a hotel coat hanger that you can take off easily, put back on and there are enough of them?

Nina Myskow

Course you might know someone like Michael Winner would have a knack of getting what he wants in hotels – probably gets as many coat hangers as he likes, hundreds of them if he wants them.

MINI BAR

Whatever you do, however low morale gets, don't open the mini bar. Everyone knows that the cost of the stuff in the mini bar is obscene. The cost of the Pringles would probably exceed the cost of the holiday itself. But hey, you can't pull the wool over our eyes: you won't find us spending £3 on a tiny bottle of mineral water from the mini bar when you can save money and lug a ton of it back to our room from the local supermarket.

I've long ago learned that you don't touch the mini bar. You look at the mini bar, you look at the chocolates in the mini bar, you look at everything, and then you laugh heartily and close the door again because they're a complete rip-off and they are used only by travelling salesmen who come back pissed from a lonely dinner and then stick their head in and, you know, spend all their money.

Nina Myskow

HOTEL HEAVEN

Some of us are lucky enough to still be enchanted with hotels, still be in love with hotels, and this we feel is an enviable quality.

I absolutely adore hotels. I'm coming over as such a pathetic creature aren't I, but I'll say it again, I absolutely adore hotels, I adore everything about them. The little 'DO NOT DISTURB' signs – I like looking at how they've done that graphically; sometimes it's a man sleeping, sometimes it's someone sort of walking about the room. Have you been in those ones where you press a button and a red or green light comes on inside your door? They're great: do not disturb, press a button and they light up. I love all that. I love the little bit of police tape they put round the toilet to show you that it's been cleaned. I lik the bed being

folded down, little chocolates, everything about them. I love
those tiny bottles of heavily diluted washing-up liquid that pass
as shower gel.

Stuart Maconie

THE CHAMBERMAIDS

The wise guest keeps in with the chambermaid. If you are stupid enough to use the sign that says 'PLEASE MAKE UP MY ROOM NOW' or mad enough to call down to reception to complain about the chambermaid, frankly you had it coming. Just don't leave your toothbrush lying around anywhere near the loo; otherwise they'll use it to clean the loo with while you're down at breakfast. It's the hotel equivalent of spitting in the pudding of someone who has complained about the food to the waiter. In fact put your toothbrush in your handbag – be on the safe side.

FOOD AND DRINK

The hotel is slightly nicer than a high-security block, your room has to be the worst one on the floor and morale is low. You've had a terrible night's sleep: the delivery vans were reversing underneath your window at 4 a.m., the dustbins were emptied shortly afterwards and the couple in the room next door took the opportunity of being woken up in the middle of the night to find something very noisy and physical to do. Only thing now is to get down to breakfast as early as possible and do some serious eating. Strip it bare single-handed and get your money's worth. You won't be hungry, but that's irrelevant. Better still, get down to breakfast the night before and bag some of it for later.

Obviously the nice fruit goes early, and the good cereal in the
boxes – that goes early so you really have to get down, better

still go the night before when they've laid out the breakfast and then, you know, ensure your supply – hide it under a sofa or something.

Arabella Weir

There's someone who's really at the top of her game, hotel-wise. Either that or get down to breakfast and really take out your disappointment about the state of the hotel on the staff downstairs, or simply just make a scene with the fruit juice, as Matthew Parris does.

What I can't stand about these modern hotel breakfasts, where you serve yourself, is there are two or three enormous generous jugs of fruit juice and dozens of tiny, tiny little glasses, no bigger than thimbles. Well, what I always do, even if I don't want much orange juice, is make a point of refilling my thimble 27 times, just to show the hotel that they can't make me drink less juice by having smaller glasses.

Matthew Parris

Once you've stripped the cereals and fruit bare, you can start on the big stuff, the cooked breakfast – what the Spanish think of as bacon or what the Turkish think of as sausage, which is more like a kebab, but hey, get it down you.

I do find myself being a bit like Alan Partridge with his big plate when I'm in these hotels. I can't help but think, It's free, I'm just going to have as much as I can fit in, so it's like, oh the fried breakfast, yeah, I'll have, yeah, three fried eggs, I think, and seven rashers of bacon and some tomato and oh, black pudding, I haven't had that for a while, and I pile it all on and spend the rest of the day sort of lying on the beach in agony because I've overdone it.

John O'Farrell

You don't even like sausages for breakfast but somehow you helped yourself to 12 of them. Point is as the holiday goes on you'll be hung-over – most British holiday makers, face it, are hung-over every morning of their holiday – and in this respect you will be thankful for those tinned tomatoes and that powdered scrambled egg. Mark my words, you will.

> *Has anyone ever with a hangover said, 'Oh, I could murder a continental breakfast'? It's just not something you hear, is it? Your beans chips sausage… the idea that anyone's going to go, 'Oh, I feel terrible, what I wouldn't give for a massive big continental breakfast, little Babyliss cheese, cold ham, that'll get me sorted.'*
>
> Stuart Maconie

You've eaten enough for the whole week but then you go and help yourself to some more. With half-board the idea is to eat up the hotel food for the whole day – buck the system. Once you've eaten so much English breakfast that you feel like going back to bed or need a lie-down, your next mission is to steal as much food as is left to use up for lunch, to get more of your money back and to get yourself a free packed lunch, sneaking it away when no one is looking into the beach bag for later. They try to prevent it with their pointless and tragic signs telling you not to take food from the restaurant, but no one takes any notice at all. Some people take so much they're probably flogging it on the beach, having opened a stall.

> *Then you have the buffet scenario on a package holiday and if you're doing half-board or whatever, and I do find myself doing this at breakfast, I take a very large bag, usually the beach bag actually, some big old beach bag and you find yourself putting bread rolls and bananas and bits of cheese in the beach bag. And I tell you, you know, pull yourself together, you*

don't even eat this stuff when it's there looking nice on a plate, do you seriously think that in four hours' time when you're on a beach and it's got bits of sand stuck to it your kids are going to eat that?

Jane Moore

Oh, breakfast buffets are meant to have things sneaked out of. I mean, I think that's why you have either a handbag with you or pockets in your shorts. And so you walk out like a gunslinger, very nonchalantly ... If you are in one of those situations where your deal is hotel, bed and breakfast and maybe dinner or something and no lunch, then of course you're going to take the bread rolls. What else are they for, with a bit of ham – why not?

Nina Myskow

If you're on half-board in a posh hotel and there's a bit of a fancy breakfast cart going on you need all the croissants you can get, frankly – all the pains au chocolat, all the yoghurts, especially if you've got kids, cos that's lunch taken care of, isn't it, really?

Kathryn Flett

I know a multi-millionaire who does this: he takes the fruit from the breakfast buffet and he takes some yoghurts from the breakfast buffet and he has them in his room on the terrace for lunch, so he gets lunch free, as it were. This is at Sandy Lane, you know, where it's £3,000 for a suite. And he's doing this to save tuppence halfpenny. I mean, people's behaviour is unbelievable.

Michael Winner

There will be distractions at breakfast, it has to be said. You will start to eye people up, and to speculate about who is going out

with who and what people do for a living, or indeed just start a
big long bitching session about everyone else. To make you feel
better, to amuse and divert you.

> *The worst thing is that I am quite deaf and I've got a loud voice
> and the combination of the two is anti-social basically,
> because what happens is at breakfast I start slagging everyone
> off and what I don't realise is that people can hear ... Look at
> the little mini slag over there with her pierced ears and Phoebe
> is going well – she's going to give me daggers now because she
> can hear every single word you are saying, you know. So I
> have to not forget that I am foghorn leghorn.*
>
> Jenny Eclair

THE INTERNATIONAL BUFFET

The evening buffet is breakfast but with absolutely no vestige of
civility at all. If you thought breakfast was a rugby scrum, wait
and watch when the king prawns come out of an evening and are
put on the buffet; watch when the (once-weekly) smoked salmon
is put out as an hors d'oeuvre. Because it's expensive and because
there is not that much of it, you want it, and the feeling is that
even if you don't want that much of it, you don't want it to get
into enemy hands. The Germans and the Russians have got it
down to a fine art. You think you are beyond caring, you think
the amount you took was cheeky, but wait and see what a full-on
middle-aged Russian woman can do with a medium-sized plate
and a serving bowl full of king prawns. She can empty them
single-handed, that's what; she can without shame pile them
high in a Jenga-type style and take them back to her large family. She will not care. Worse, she won't eat them all or half of
them. But the point is she will be in possession of them, and
that's what counts when it comes to buffets. It'll be all you can

International Buffet

do not to actually pull up a chair and sit down in front of it all, saving yourself the trouble of lugging it all back to your table.

> *They pile their plates, they can't even carry this plate it's so full. It's so silly, cos they can go back for more anyway; they don't have to pile their plate. They're not only allowed one visit to the buffet, and then 'You're banned you came ten minutes ago'. I don't do that, you know. I'm too fat anyway, so I tend to limit my intake.*

> Michael Winner

It's not even as if international buffets are that appetising. Or even appetising at all.

> *I hate buffets, on the whole, I mean, part of me, the greedy part of me, is, ooh yummy, all this food, I can eat whatever I*

like, but at the same time I think all these things have been sitting there congealing, you know – scrambled eggs that have been there since pre-dawn, they look like the primeval swamps.

Nina Myskow

International buffets. Yes, so called. International, because they're the same the world over, not because they in any way represent any stab at internationalism. It is that thing, the all-you-can-eat-for concept, isn't it? Particularly at those all-inclusive resorts, where you've paid your money up front and it's all free. So, pile as much as you can on your plate, and another plate, and another plate, and then get that on a tray and then get your butt over to the bar for the extremely watered-down cocktail, because clearly you've paid x amount up front.

Kathryn Flett

Some people rise above it all. Or say they do.

I love that slightly racy feeling of not bothering with breakfast – you know, the hell with it, let their £11.50 go hang, I know I've paid for it, I just … I'm a sucker for hotels. I could go and stay in a hotel, have a great holiday staying in a hotel like on a ring road somewhere on the outskirts of, you know, Telford. I just love it, just love everything about it – opening the door, getting my free Financial Times that I never read. It's all a glamorous world to me.

Stuart Maconie

One of Britain's hotel chains has decided to offer pets their very own beds. The hotel says the move is aimed at customers who cannot bear to be parted from their cats and dogs. The special 2ft 6in long pet beds will be tried out at hotels around the country. It comes after a survey of customers showed almost two-thirds hated leaving their pets behind when they were away from home.

In fact I think I might have stayed in one of those dog beds myself.

ENTERTAINMENT

The hotel has laid on some excellent entertainment in the bar: a fabulous Englebert Humperdinck look-alike, probably an *X Factor* runner-up, or *Opportunity Knocks* more like, and it's all pumping out at top volume, which is distressing because he's got a karaoke machine, so things aren't going to get any better. Hotel entertainment is a bad sign for the grumpy holiday maker; in fact the two words together send a bit of a chill down me. Anything that involves an entertainment officer or entertainment team, or, God forbid, anyone organising entertainment who has a whistle round their neck, or a noticeboard at reception with an entertainment programme on it, and frankly you might as well just change hotels the moment you get there, because this is going to be very challenging indeed.

LOLLING

Stay in a hotel and you can do some serious lolling, some full-on I'm-going-to-take-it-easy time. Close the door, slob out, do nothing, waste time – marvellous. That's what I call a holiday: please yourself, make a mess, no, make a really big mess, and no one cares, no one knows – you can do what you like.

FREEBIES

The other pastime to amuse you in hotels is to stash away the stuff you are going to take home with you. Your own little 'free' stash of souvenirs.

You've paid for the room, and you've probably paid through the nose for the room, so logically you are allowed to take some of it home with you. It's expected of you; the nicer the hotel the more they expect you to take. More like want you to take. We get carried away – why stop at the shower cap? Anything that's not nailed down and you can carry past reception goes in – you'll take anything, OK then, not anything.

I'm afraid I'm one of those people who regards myself as entitled to everything in the entire room if I've paid for it: lamps, desks, I mean, if I could I'd, you know, I'd strip the room, because you think, well, I did pay £75 for it, I'm entitled to all the fixtures and fittings. The really clever thing to do when you're stealing the stuff from a hotel is actually to get the trolley the maid leaves in the hall. When she's in another room you can just empty the trolley like that of all the sachets of hot chocolate and everything. That's when you're really on your game, when you're at your best; at the top of your game that's what you do, you empty the trolley out into your bag.

Arabella Weir

It's not nicking toiletries, is it? It is there for you to help yourself to really. I mean, they leave it there and if you are there for a couple of weeks and you put it in your bag every day and they refill it every day then, you know, it's up to them. You mean they are not there for you to take? I thought that you were supposed to take them, if there was a robe in your room and slippers, and pillows and the sofa and the telly.

Linda Robson

Oh, obviously the posher the hotel, the more stuff there is to have. And I think they built that in, really. I mean, when you stay in a really posh hotel and they have the robes and the slippers and they have that little note attached to the robe and it says, you know, 'If you enjoy wearing this robe,' or words to that effect, 'then why not pick up one in our shop?' – you think, yes, why not just pick up this one?

Kathryn Flett

I am not interested in the robe, you know. I have a manager, he is obsessed with the robe – I mean, he phones me up from hotels, talks about the robe, the robe, the robe, the robe, I've got a robe, I'm going to take the robe. I don't get it, I don't have robe envy, you know. The robes are big. I never looked attractive in a huge terry-towelling dressing gown; I think it's only a large fit man that looks good in it. I always think that when you look in Hello magazine, couples with children who wear towelling dressing gowns to be photographed are making a huge mistake. It's a very unflattering item.

Rhona Cameron

I am over the slippers. So over the complimentary flippy-floppy slippers that make you trip up as you walk.

I am addicted to the hotel slipper. I do wear them at home and whoever I am with goes, 'That depressing big strange dirty hotel slipper – must you wear it? At least wear them both.' No, so I have slippers on with my socks and I seem to be quite addicted to them.

Rhona Cameron

What's encouraging, though, is that someone as rich and as in your face as Michael Winner has been known to nick a few freebies. And even has been known to be caught out. Even better.

I do remember once in Paris years ago when I was still a student I was at a very posh hotel and I took the towels, the bathroom towels and the bathroom coats, and I left the hotel, got in a taxi and it stopped at the lights and I could see in the mirror the manager running from the hotel down to the lights to get to my car. He got to my car and he said, 'Excuse me, Mr Winner,' he said, 'we think you may have inadvertently taken something from the room. Could we look in your suitcase?' And he looked in this suitcase, taking out towels, more towels, bathrobes, flannels, but he said, 'Don't worry, Mr Winner, a lot of people do it,' he said, but that taught me my lesson. I only now take minor objects and I always tell them.

Michael Winner

SELF-CATERING OPTION

Alternatively you can shun the hotel and do your own thing – rent a villa or a country cottage, be independent. This sort of holiday too, it has to be said, has its potential disappointments, and tragically when things don't come up to scratch there's not even someone at reception to go and have a good old rant at to get it off your chest.

We rented a place once in Cornwall that was so damp... It wasn't near the sea and it was in a sort of hollow. It made it look from the brochure like it was in a sort of woody glade but what it was actually in was a sort of hollow that was reminiscent of Deliverance, so it was just all sort of dark leaves and in-breds and stuff. I'm not suggesting everybody in Cornwall is an in-bred; I'm just saying that in that area that's what it felt like. I just wanted to sit on the porch with a loaded gun all night.

Arabella Weir

Forget the shampoo ...

Gone are the days of just taking the toiletries or even the bath robe. Brits are becoming greedier with their holiday steals. Countless holiday makers are leaving their hotel rooms with mirrors, light fittings, curtains, doorknobs and some even managed to get away with the carpet.

The top five bizarre items left behind in a hotel in one year were:

- Prosthetic legs
- Ferrari keys
- A Last Will & Testament
- Bridget Jones-style knickers
- Thirty Power Ranger dolls

The top ten items left in a room were:

- Mobile phone and chargers
- Clothing items
- Toiletries
- False teeth
- Laptops
- Electrical gadgets such as iPods and digital cameras
- Cash or credit cards
- Jewellery or watches
- Hen/stag night accessories
- Keys

The other potential problem with self-catering is, frankly, who is it in the party who is going to be doing the catering? Self is the keyword here. Self-catering means if you don't do it no one else will, basically. Which means if you're a grumpy old woman you might just as well have stopped at home.

> *You start sort of bearing up a mental grudge list, where you start thinking, well, OK, it's fine, everyone's on holiday and we're all in the same boat, and it would just be really nice if somebody else put some eggs on to boil for packed lunch, that would be really nice, but it's me, isn't it? It's always me. And then you sort of get slightly more and more het up and you sort of ... It's just basically a bit like being at home but with different pots and pans, and you just start to resent it quite badly.*
>
> *Jenny Eclair*

And self-catering places are never very child friendly, are they? Or they never have enough pans or enough dish cloths, and you have to go out to the supermarket and buy everything, even a packet of salt. It's all rather hard work really, which can lead to a top-of-the-range grump on holiday – be warned.

> *When you are a parent of small babies, you think, wouldn't it be a good idea to go away and rent a little cottage in the country somewhere? Because you've got your house sorted out as safe as you want it for the children, with a fire guard and plug covers and a baby gate on the stairs, you think, let's go somewhere where there's a spitting open fire with a sort of special trip point right in front of it where there's electric wires sticking out from the side of all the plugs, and where there are really steep concrete stairs that your baby keeps heading for every thirty seconds.*
>
> *John O'Farrell*

4

Camping

You can see the appeal: the great outdoors, back to nature, getting in touch with your inner self, the simple life. There was a camping trip once in your distant childhood memory which was fun, or someone persuaded you it was fun; you thought that cooking a sausage and some beans outdoors was the most thrilling thing that had ever happened to you; someone else (probably Akela) lit a campfire and you sang some jolly songs; you didn't notice how far it was to the loo, you didn't have a shower in the shower block because when you were eight you didn't wash at all – and so you want to recreate it, probably with your own children, and you take a camping holiday.

Now the possibilities for disappointment and grump are really stacking up. Your memory has played a cruel trick on you. The last time you camped was when you were twelve and someone else, probably Akela again, or Brown Owl, did all the zips and poles and tent pegs. Now it's like your worst self-assembly Ikea nightmare, but with the added tension of a raging storm brewing, or like being a refugee without the United

Nations to bail you out with helicopter food drops or shelter.

OK, some people's memories haven't played tricks on them.

I did all that when I was a child and I just want comfort now, I don't want crispy bog roll in the campsite toilets and I don't want to queue with some other family to use the loo and I want my comforts, you know. I work very hard, so therefore why would I want to go on holiday and have a worse standard of living than I do at home? I don't get that. People go, 'Oh, you know, where's your sense of adventure?' and you just think, get a grip. It's just that kind of thing so people can go, 'Well, yeah, you know, it was just really hard and we trekked and we camped on the side of a mountain and we didn't get much sleep but hey, it was, it was great,' and you just think, Liar, liar.

Jane Moore

Holidays weren't annoying when we were young. We frolicked, we scampered, we spent the whole day damming a stream or making a sandcastle, even in Prestatyn; life was innocent and perfect. And you're so keen to recapture those heady, carefree holidays you decide, oh, what fun it would be to go camping. You have a perfectly comfortable home of your own with proper beds and a cooker and running water and everything, but adventure beckons.

Camping is more popular than ever. Amazingly, the Camping and Caravanning Club of Great Britain has half a million members, and on 24 May 2003 there were 92,450 people camping in Britain alone. (For some reason that was the day they counted.)

This phrase 'getting back to nature' – I don't want to get back to nature, I don't want to hunt rabbits and eat raw flesh with my bare hands, you know. I want to get as far away from nature as possible. I want to sit in a nice restaurant where somebody else has cooked you a nice meal and you eat it with a knife and fork, thank you very much, with a roof over my head. What is the point of getting back to nature, apart from getting wet and then being eaten by a mammoth? No thanks.

John O Farrell

Of course, if you like spending a fortnight crawling around on your hands and knees, then camping is definitely for you; and it's especially for you if you like tripping over the tent pegs and then having to walk half a mile to the nearest loo or, if it's in the middle of the night, which it inevitably will be, enjoy weeing in the bushes.

It is easy for blokes because they're far from the ground, but you're not, you're very close to the ground and you're not able to run away because you've got your knickers round your ankles, so should something untoward occur like a snake coming up and biting you on the bottom, which is entirely possible, or some nasty creepy-crawly sort of jumping at you, you can't run – all you would do would be kind of topple face forward.

Nina Myskow

My father had the right line on camping. He would always say, 'It's contrived poverty, contrived poverty. Why would you go to that much trouble to live in poverty?' and he's right. We spent a hundred thousand years as homo sapiens, learning to build basic shelters, then learning to put running water in them, learning to have a fire to keep them warm. Let me go, 'I know, why don't we all go off and live under canvas like refugees in sub-Sahara Africa? And, you know, have butter with ants crawling in it and have water dripping into the, you know, soggy mildewy sleeping bag and everyone goes "Isn't

this lovely?" No, it's not lovely, why would I want to choose to
live like that?

John O Farrell

I really don't ever want to go camping ever again. I don't, you
know. I was brought up to be very, very hardy and now I
just want fluffy towels and hot water. I do not want to try
and have dinner over one bloody gas ring. It's sort of invented
for Scottish people, I think, like porridge, people who don't
like to have a good time, people who know the value of a
pound.

Arabella Weir

I must say I drove past a campsite in the south of France, sited on
something that looked like a swamp, not so long ago, and I
assumed it must be a refugee camp. I was genuinely shocked
when someone pointed out it was full of holiday makers in tents.
In fact it would be hard for an alien to come up with some serious differences between a campsite and a refugee camp. Perhaps
the odd foldaway table and chairs or the odd bottle of mineral
water might give it away, but you'd be hard pushed. And of
course this might be the problem with camping. Camping on the
side of a lake in a secluded mountain stream on your own, with
just the car as a getaway, might be appealing, even stunningly
wonderful if the weather was good, but it's campsites, not the
camping itself, that are so irritating – and of course the dreaded
phenomenon of other people, which is the real problem with
camping. And, let's face it, on a campsite your neighbours are
seriously too close for comfort. You can hear them snoring at
night, and a lot more if you're unlucky.

The four-man tent is more like a four-toddler tent. You have so
little personal space that even the most solid of relationships
start to crack under the strain. Except of course having an argu-

ment in a tent in a campsite is unthinkable if you want to look your neighbours in the eye the next day. Sooner or later it occurs to you how long would it take to drive home, but that would be admitting defeat.

> *Now I'm at the age where I think that's kind of rugged and macho, but it's only been relatively recently that I've got into that sort of stuff. Until I was about 25 if I went somewhere that didn't have a microwave I thought that was camping, you know. If I went somewhere that didn't have gin and tonics, I thought that was camping and I just thought, people were insane who would willingly give up, you know, solid architectural features like doors, for just kind of rolling around in a canvas bag in some farmer's field.*
>
> Stuart Maconie

Truth is camping these days has taken a different direction. Nowadays the idea is to make your tent as much like a house as possible, with walls and rooms and kitchens and tellies. Which is surely not the point.

The ideal place for camping – it seems to me – is your own back garden. That way you can get the feeling of living en plein air but still be within reach of your own flushing loos and a power shower and Sky Plus for when it rains. You know it makes sense.

CAMPING WITH TEENAGERS

There's only one thing worse than camping in the sleet and rain and that's camping with teenage kids. It's as much as they can do to summon up the effort to keep their flip-flops on; they can't even be bothered with shoes, never mind getting out for a nice bracing walk or putting on any rambling gear – or even a coat.

My parents went in for a lot of bracing walks, 'cos it's good for
you, 'cos if you are Scottish anything that's horrible is good for
you, and so there were a lot of bracing walks in the rain, and
you know you're not getting supper until you've walked eight
miles up the Cairngorms.

Arabella Weir

SCOTLAND

Scotland – ah yes … It's the mother ship of camping, mission control of outdoor-type holidays. On paper it looks irresistible – dramatic scenery, heather, lochs, craggy mountains, shops with
really classy souvenirs and some nice tartan and bagpipes – but
having fun on a Scottish holiday is for people who like a challenge. The challenge of the midge.

The weather in Scotland, in case you are not familiar with it,
is unspeakable: the scenery is breathtaking, but basically the
story is winter; and then in August when the sun does come out
and the place is basking in the most amazing light imaginable,
the midges come out in such numbers that you see people out for
a nice early evening walk with netting over their faces, fishing-
net-type things on upside down as protection. They look as if
they've been dealing with Chernobyl.

Summer of seventy-six, a very hot summer, everyone who's
old enough to remember will recall. Even in Scotland,
absolutely blistering, but obviously this weather brought out
some sort of new strain of supermidge in the Western Isles,
which meant that you were effectively fighting your way
through clouds of the little bastards every time the sun went
down and you wanted to have that relaxing moment round
the campfire. So that was quite stressful, it was difficult. But
yes, Scotland is sort of good in theory. I have Scottish genes

and Scottish kind of skin and it works for me. The rain's nice, lots of good brisk walks, yep. It's not the Caribbean, though, is it?

Kathryn Flett

It's bracing, which is holiday-speak for freezing and really cold and wet and dangerous. It is invigorating, but that's what, you know, it's like. You see, Scotland, bracing weather, you've got to make your own fun, great pop music, great comedy ... The weather is appalling but it's had a shaping effect on the national character.

Stuart Maconie

I admire people who walk the Scottish mountains with some stupid old gnarled stick and a kilt, but not me, thank you.

Michael Winner

Scotland on holiday – never. I lived there and it was like a cold purgatory. I mean, why on earth would anybody go to Scotland on holiday? There's the one day in the year when the sun shines and then you're eaten alive by midges. It's ... People talk about scenery, but you can buy, you can rent a video and watch scenery. I have got drenched in Scotland, I have got drizzled on in Scotland, I have had wind blown – I mean, I've got broken veins on my face from, you know, wind coming off the beach in St Andrews. I mean, it is just a repellent place.

Nina Myskow

CARAVANS

There is another way, for people who really can't be doing with this level of discomfort and downright inconvenience. Here's an idea: take a little house away on holiday with you, tow it behind you for six hours on the dual carriageway. It'd be like having your own shed on holiday, and grumpy people like sheds.

> *You see, it's like a mini home and I like that. You're near people but they're not in such close proximity and I love that. I find the rain on the caravan roof a very comforting sound and I've often thought perhaps I should live in a caravan and, you know, I think I'd be quite happy there, I'd love the caravan. I don't know what to say – I've nothing but good things to say about it. It's a shame that it's been labelled with, you know, the old trailer trash thing because I'd quite happily live in a caravan park.*
>
> *As a child I grew up on caravan club holidays and you knew you were all in the caravan club because you would toot your horn on the motorway and wave and the family would wave back and there'd be a little flag sticking out the back of the caravan with 'CC' on it, which meant caravan club.*
>
> *It was very innocent and then you'd always buy a little badge or a teaspoon with a little crest on it to represent the place that you visited and you put it in your large teaspoon drawer with all the other little crests, and then one day perhaps when it was raining if you weren't going outside you'd get out your teaspoons and look through the crests. In the days before the Internet.*
>
> Rhona Cameron

OK, so you have a bit more room to swing your rucksack than in a two-man tent, but it has to be said that even caravan holidays are designed for small people, like children who like playing in their teeny weeny Wendy house with a teeny weeny sink and a teeny weeny cooker. It's really rather cute, and there is a bit of me that finds the whole business of your little miniature home and miniature world rather appealing, rather liberating, in the sense that you can whizz around and tidy up in two seconds flat, you are self-contained, you can go anywhere you like. Well, I say you can go anywhere you like, yes, of course you can … Trouble is you can only park caravans in campsites, so you are back to square one.

For the family of four who even at home in a proper house get in each other's way and invade one another's space, I can guarantee that with caravanning by day two – no, I will revise that and say lunchtime of day one – you'll all be getting on each other's nerves. Morale is low, and even a second game of Monopoly or Snakes and Ladders doesn't do it. You do have the fabulously convenient loo built in, fair dos. Bit too convenient perhaps, in that it is about six inches away from the dining area. Nice.

With a tent basically the idea is to go to the pub and get so drunk you don't really notice having to crawl in through the tent in the cold and damp and get yourself zipped up in the sleeping bag as fast as possible and hope that you don't need the loo until it's light, which naturally will be a hope in vain; but with caravans the whole business of getting the house into sleep mode, and getting shutters and shelves and perches and catches and cushions rearranged into bedroom mode, is something best done sober. Even if you have the foresight to do this before you go to the pub, you'll come home from the pub and still find you have to get on to some sort of shelf on a ladder designed for four-year-olds, and yes, OK, you won't have to go outside when you need the loo in the night, but you will have to somehow roll over on your perch and reverse down the ladder designed for four-year-olds in the dark. Perhaps this sort of caper should be restricted by law to the under-12s.

My parents owned a Sprite 400. Now this is a type of caravan and I think it was called a Sprite 400 because it was only big enough for sprites: it was the smallest caravan in the world. It was one of those caravans that thinks it's oh so clever because the only table turns into a double bed and it doesn't really and then you sort of have two sort of hanging things like hammocky bits ... They were shelves actually, they were two shelves that my sister and I slept on, so you'd have the kitchen table that turned into a double bed for my mother and father, and then my sister and I would be tucked into shelves. I think, you know, my mother tried to put a brave face on it and she was sort of about eight months pregnant with my brother, and it was very hot that year and I seem to remember her putting vodka on her cornflakes to start the day off.

Jenny Eclair

CAMPERVANS

Unfortunately caravans and campervans, which are just caravans on wheels, lull you into a false sense of security, temperature and comfort-wise, because they have things that remind you of solid architectural features like doors and windows and you assume that they are going to be rain and wind proof. Last time I was in a campervan, and I suspect it will be the last time, was at Easter (I was thinking early spring sun, nice long evenings) on the north-east coast. It was so cold I slept in my clothes, a huge padded coat, my hat and then a duvet and then the towels from the bathroom. I still woke up freezing cold. Then I noticed why I was so cold: the little cosy gas fire in the 'living' area had a hole directly out to the open air, revealing a view of grass beneath – obviously a ventilation hole for the gas fire. The problem with campervans, like tents and caravans, is that even though they look as if they are the ultimate freedom-holiday-in-a-vehicle idea, truth is that you can't park them anywhere. Except for about three places per county, and then as with caravans you are back to square one, because on the whole

Every time I wake
up and open the curtains,
I think we're still in that
traffic jam on the M5

either you are on a lay-by on the A38, risking life and limb every
time a juggernaut goes past, making new best friends with
truckers and greasy spoon cafés and wondering what it is they
do when the curtains in their cab are drawn at two in the afternoon, or – guess what – you're in a campsite.

OUTDOOR PURSUITS

With holidays in Britain, the thing is to move about a lot; inertia,
unless there is a heatwave, is not really an option. There are hills
to climb, mountains to be conquered, fells to run up, cagoules to

wear, sopping wet sandwiches to dry out. You get the air in your lungs, you feel on top of the world. It's the great British pastime of rambling – OK, walking about a bit.

> *I hate the term rambling because it implies little thermos in the Cotswolds, you know, in a phalanx of people whose best days are basically behind them, shall we put it like that? You know what I mean, collecting postcards of local interest, with perhaps a cream tea at the end of the day.*
>
> Stuart Maconie

Cream teas – now you're talking. That's what we call a holiday.

BAD WEATHER ON BRITISH HOLIDAYS

A bad caravan holiday and frankly you had it coming: bad weather on holiday is unavoidable, especially in Britain. In fact a British holiday wouldn't be the same without the rain: you'd feel cheated if it didn't rain, sheets of it. It's why God invented pacamacs and made Kendal mint cake shower proof.

But this is where all those fabulous rainy day attractions come into their own. There are hundreds of lovely rainy day attractions and activities to immerse yourself in. Like for instance the Pencil Museum in Keswick. It's not like it's just pencils: it's different-coloured pencils, it's different-sized pencils. Pencils you can pencil with, even.

> *The Pencil Museum in Keswick must have, you know, oh, they must look out of the window every day at the Pencil Museum and go, 'Ooh, look at that, you can see the isobars, huddling together. We've got five days of continuous rain and storms coming – kerching.'*
>
> Stuart Maconie

All over the English countryside are these brown signs that well, as you get older all kinds of things that when you are young and more sensible are just unattractive – when you get older you start to get into all kinds of things; all sorts of leisure activities start to take on an appeal. Like going to see local churches – that might be quite fun. It's not, but I think you get to a certain age where you convince yourself that you can't just drink 80 Bacardi Breezers and lie in the street and that's a holiday.

Stuart Maconie

I've done some research into other wonderful rainy day attractions in the UK, lest you are silly enough to go on a camping holiday when the weather is wet. Here are some positively worth making a note of:

- Savings Banks Museum in Scotland: you can see books on the history of savings banks.
- Soap Museum in Cornwall: I can hear you all getting your coats on now to make your way there. Might be best to book.
- Type and Font Museum in London: discover the history of Times New Roman and Courier New at the leading international font museum.
- Carpet Museum in Kidderminster: a travelling museum that boasts such sell-out events as the lecture 'Kidderminster to Vegas via Singapore – the Revelations of a Carpet Designer'.

Or further afield:

- There's the Celery Interpretive Centre in Michigan, which promises a detailed history of the continued growth of celery, including a 1931 elevator. You never know when you might find all this incredibly useful.
- Or how about the Jerusalem Tax Museum, where you can learn about the routine work of tax departments to your

heart's content?

- Or the Fan Museum in London, with an astonishing 3,000 fans to admire.
- The Salt Museum in Northwich has pretty much everything you ever wanted to know about salt, and presumably a great deal more besides.

5
Children

Taking a small child on holiday is a nice abstract concept, but by definition it invariably means taking a child *travelling*. It might – and I know you don't want to think about it – mean taking a child on a *long* car journey, and believe me children and long car journeys are not a great start to a holiday, even if you have one of those gas-guzzling four-wheel drives with brilliant little mini TV screens on the backs of the front seats for them to watch, even if you give them sedatives or buy up the whole of the pick-and-mix counter in Woollies. Believe me, a long car journey with small children is going to get the holiday off to a seriously bad start.

There are only so many games of I-spy a family can play on the M5, and then you will have to move on to spotting police cars or red lorries, and then when they're fed up of that, you will have to go back to I-spy. You might even in a long motorway-roadworks queue have to resort to seeing who can make their jelly baby last the longest. Get the picture? And as anyone who has been foolish enough to not take seriously a child who says they feel sick in the back of a car will (now) know, travelling with small children can be at best tedious and at worst a test of unconditional love. Either that or they sleep the entire way and you get to the hotel in deepest Devon after a day's work, loading up the car and the journey from hell, and they wake up refreshed and alert and are awake till 3 a.m., bright as a button and wanting to play.

No, as anyone who has ever holidayed with a small baby or child knows, a holiday with children is not a holiday at all but childminding without the aid of Bob the Builder tapes and with the added complication of heat rash, jellyfish stings and an inevitable need for first aid. Much as we all love our children, holidays with them when they're small are entirely devoid of all the things you liked doing on holiday before you were a parent – reading, lolling on a sunbed, sex, relaxation, losing track of time, watching a sunset on a beach ... Well, yes, I suppose you can do those things, as long as you take it in turns, and then that will only really work if you have one child, and not really with the sex bit.

You could pack the little darlings off to the hotel's mini club, the one in which the brochure said your child would be busy with creative play from morning till night, the one it said you would have to prise him away from at the end of the fortnight – well, you could pack them off there; but nobody does, because the entertainment programme on offer is basically colouring in and, nice as colouring in is (and as an adult I could be jolly happy doing something as straightforward as colouring in), colouring in for a week is enough to send any child running back to their parents and wanting to be dunked in the pool, to have castles dug in the sand, to go rockpooling or to have a ride on a banana boat. Which is sort of the point: since the people who run kids clubs are the holiday equivalent of a Saturday girl – completely unin-terested in children, hopelessly hung over and unspeakably bored – the point of the kiddies club is that it closes down because of lack of interest and lack of other kids, and that means that the parents on the poolside are left to run water polo games, diving competitions and treasure hunts of their own. Which is nice, for a bit, but when you've been working your arse off to pay for the trip you need some serious relaxation, and relaxation is distressingly hard to achieve on holiday with small children.

Unless of course you can afford to take the nanny on holiday – and if you can I can tell you from experience the chances are you will be resentful to the point of being beetroot in the face the moment she takes her T-shirt off on the beach and looks drop dead gorgeous in her sliver of a bikini. No, if you do decide to holiday with small children – and frankly leaving them behind is both impractical and understandably illegal – you have to choose very different holidays from the ones you were used to taking as a childless couple.

Believe me, I know. Our first holiday with a baby was to the kind of place we would ordinarily have gone to pre-baby. It didn't occur to us to do anything else. We went to an apartment in a villa on a hill overlooking a stunning bay in Crete, off the beaten track. 'Off the beaten track' once you have small children no longer means quiet and gorgeously secluded: it means a long way to the nearest hospital when a child has cut their forehead open on the hideously sharp corner of a glass coffee table in your apartment's kitchenette, or run into the plate-glass window on the terrace which doesn't have any warning markings on the outside, or slipped on the newly washed marble floor in the restaurant. And a villa on a hill means that you spend every waking hour watching your toddler in case he or she wanders for a nanosecond near the pool boundary, from which there is a 300-foot drop which has only some bougainvillea bushes to save their fall.

Other, childless, unsympathetic couples lolled endlessly on their sunbeds, having monopolised the shade, while we sterilised bottles, administered Calpol and soothed teething pains exacerbated by it being 90 degrees in the shade. Dealing with a fractious small baby in a villa in the small hours, with only a limited supply of Calpol and no video games to calm them down, is properly hard work. Childless, unsympathetic couples look on in pity at parents who are trying hard to entertain their small kids and watch them disapprovingly splashing in the pool or playing with a ball; then they have a nice glass of white wine for lunch and saunter indoors (having chained the sun umbrellas to their sun-loungers) for an afternoon rest, which is code for some afternoon nookie, while you are desperately trying to keep a small child from boiling over in the heat or an overactive toddler from running around the pool and tripping to their death. Sometimes I felt like saying, 'Look, couldn't you lot just take turns with us for an hour – give us an hour off? I mean, it's not like you're busy or anything.'

Truth is once you have children there are two schools of thought. Either you book a holiday that is geared totally around them; the bucket-and-spade holiday is the obvious one – grit your teeth and go to St Ives for a fortnight, brave the pixie shops when it rains, go for a bracing walk on the seafront somewhere. Or you holiday on regardless and take the hideously exhausting consequences of taking a small child abroad. Some people even take small children on long-haul holidays. Once. It's not the sort of mistake you make twice. If you do, maybe the best plan would be to seat them in a different bit of the plane.

I have heard of people, famous people off the telly, and I know of one for definite who sits in first class but put their kids in economy and then their excuse is that they don't want to inflict their children on other first-class payers, and you go, 'Why is it all right to inflict them on people in economy?'

Arabella Weir

You certainly don't want to go down the road of too much consultation with children about what sort of holiday you go on, that's for sure. That way lies – well, Disney, I suppose.

> *We don't believe that our children have a say in anything until they are in a position to pay for it, so it's just like, 'Are you paying for this holiday? No, right, well shut up then. This is where we're going. If you don't want to come to somewhere with sun, sea and sand you can stay at home.'*
>
> Jane Moore

I'm not convinced that children need holidays in the first place. Life, surely, is one long holiday when you're a kid. I blame the schools. Why do they have to close for so long in the summer break anyway?

Parents are collectively expected to spend an amazing £7.6 billion keeping their children entertained during the summer holiday. The average family will spend just over £590 keeping their children amused during the school break. Parents can expect to spend an average of nearly £80 on special days out, such as visits to theme parks, cinemas or the zoo.

There's no rest for parents on holiday. Children don't really do just chilling out and sitting still: they don't need to sit still, they don't need to chill out. As a parent, and probably especially as a dad, your duty is to amuse your children on holiday at all times. You wear yourself out so much that you'll be asleep before they are; they'll still be awake at 6 a.m. and they can't even wander downstairs on their own to put the telly on for an hour.

*What I find when I get in the swimming pool, I do that thing
of letting the kids climb on me and chucking them across the
water and picking them up and chucking them across again,
and then you've got these other dads who cannot be bothered
at all and they're just lying there asleep reading* Men's Health
*magazine or whatever and their kids start to gravitate
towards me cos I look like I'm fun. They say, 'Will you throw
me across the water?' I go, 'OK,' and throw that kid. Another
kid: 'Will you throw me across the water?' 'OK,' and I'm
bloody exhausted and these kids are going, 'He's fun, he lets
me hit him hard with the plastic beach mat,' and so I end up,
you know, bruised and cast as Mr Fun for the rest of the holiday. So, you know, I end up going to the pool of the hotel next
door.*

John O'Farrell

The trouble is children on holiday don't want to do the things you
expect them to want to do. They don't like doing the things I liked
doing on holiday when I was a kid. I would enjoy a holiday in
Cornwall or Devon with some ten-year-olds if they wanted to
have a lot of outdoor fun, wanted Famous-Five-type adventures
and shared my enthusiasm for fresh air, a bike ride and a picnic.
For me there is little more exciting than a picnic; I can barely contain my enthusiasm when having a Scotch egg and a bag of crisps
in the open air, I find a bike ride hugely enjoyable: it makes me
feel free, like a carefree ten-year-old all over again. I adore the
sea air; I love to paddle in the sea. But the truth is that kids take
an enormous amount of bribing, cajoling and persuasion to get
into the outdoors unless they are driven there, have their iPods
and can get back to the hotel room for *Neighbours*. They might
do a teeny weeny walk from car park to beach, they might kick
around a ball for a bit, but some good adventures with a treasure hunt and a picnic at the end are done mostly to humour me.

It's not that kids on holidays don't like danger – they seek that out like a heat-seeking missile – but they don't seem to like adventure the way I did when I was on holiday as a kid.

They still manage to do exactly the thing you dreaded them doing: hire a pedalo and they will insist on taking it right out to sea and jumping off it, or sliding down the slide, right into a busy shipping lane; find a beach next to a cliff and they will insist on climbing the rock face when your back is turned. They don't think about sunblock or rip tides or dodgy blokes on the beach, so if you want a job as a bodyguard, once the nest is empty, as a parent who has taken children on holiday and returned with them in one piece you will be extremely well qualified.

Course I can't read anyway, cos I've got children, so I've got to be constantly monitoring the sea for man-eating sharks. It's all so relaxing on holiday.

Arabella Weir

There are silver linings – advantages of having small children with you on holiday. No, really, there are …

There are many joys to having children. The biggest joy to having children is that once they are three years old you give them 50p at five o'clock in the morning and you send them down-stairs before the Germans get there to book the sun-loungers.

Jenni Trent Hughes

But children don't do sightseeing, don't do interesting, or relaxing, or exquisitely luxurious. They like spending their holiday money in hideous souvenir shops; they like playing table football or ping-pong, or doing things that involve a lot of standing up and counting score. They like canoeing, or white water rafting, or jumping up and down in the waves, or learning to surf. All these things require courage and patience, neither of which I have.

There's only one thing worse than children on holiday, and that's holidaying with other people's children, who are especially annoying, splashing and screaming and generally having a nice time and ruining your peace and quiet. Sometimes, if you have just the one child, you take other people's children on holiday with you. Which is good. Ish.

You have to take other people's children with you because your daughter is so lonely that she has her holiday face. There's nothing worse than the holiday face of the only child. You see them in hotels and on beaches all over and it peaks at about 12, when they just have this utterly haunted expression of misery and loneliness. They just palpate with loneliness – you can sort of smell it on them and despair, It's the despair of the only child being stuck with middle-aged parents.

Jenny Eclair

I suppose you could make holidaying an adult-only thing. Really go over the top. There are (childless) people who would advocate such action.

Children should not be allowed to go on holiday. They scream, they shout, they yell. You're sitting in beautiful peaceful surroundings and they're screaming, they're running, they're kicking footballs. All children should be locked up until the age of ten, and only selected ones should be let out when they're ten. They are the biggest deterrent to a holiday, children.

Michael Winner

DISNEY

Of course the other solution to the problem would be to channel all the families on holiday with small children into one big massive holiday campus, as far away as possible from anything architecturally or geographically of interest, hem them in, wall them in, charge them a fortune, make it absolutely irresistible to children so that it is habit forming and make them stay there all day every day – no doubt thousands enjoy it and thought the wait worthwhile. Oh, sorry, such a place already exists. It's called Disney.

For some of us visiting nuclear power plants in Latvia might be a better holiday than Disney. Kids or no kids, we draw the line at queuing to go on a pretend pirate cruise to see a plastic crocodile come out of the pretend swamp and squirt water at you. But sometimes the kids get to you, nag you into taking them, and you're drawn in to the heady notion of fun-filled family quality time: you give in and you decide to do the family holiday of a lifetime – splash out and go to the magical kingdom, the wonderful world of Disney.

Trouble with Disney is that it is relentlessly cheerful, relentlessly smiley. That's the point of it. Anything that tries this hard to make you cheery and happy just makes you more grumpy than normal. It all makes you so cross you might make a scene. People dressed up as Goofy and silly streets looking like Hollywood sets, 'Drip, Drip, Drop, Little April Showers' endlessly playing in the loos – nothing but joy and happiness wherever you look. It's making me come out in a grumpy sort of rash just thinking about it.

And the more they play the cheery music, the more fed up you feel. Still, at least you don't have to work there, and listen to it all day.

> *I couldn't think of anything worse than going down for break-*
> *fast and somebody interrupting me in a stupid voice with a*
> *cartoon voice. Oh, fuck off, I couldn't be doing with that, no.*
> *If I had a fork … don't come anywhere near me at breakfast,*
> *I've got a fork, you're pretending to be a cartoon character. It's*
> *only going to end in tears.*
>
> Jenny Eclair

It's like trudging round Ikea on a bank holiday, but hotter and less fun, which of course isn't saying a lot. It's a wonder there isn't more Disney rage. Trouble is everyone else – non-grumpy people, ordinary people – seems to be having such a wonderful time. Maybe it's an elaborate conspiracy … Maybe everyone tells themselves they love it and convinces themselves they are having a marvellous time for the sake of the kids. The only consolation is that other parents have been mad enough to agree to it too.

It's not even as if you can dip in and out of Disney for the odd hour. Disney being what it is – at the back end of beyond – and being as expensive as it is, you have to turn up at the crack of dawn to get your money's worth. You've flown halfway round the world to get there, but you're not much in the mood, frankly; you've probably got jet lag, you're knackered and the whole process of getting into the theme park is another long-haul journey in itself. You have to park your car, get a shuttle bus from the car to the shuttle bus, then get the monorail from the shuttle bus to the boat, and then cruise over the lake to the gates and get a shuttle from the gates to the entrance – you're worn out before you get there. It's hot, the kids are already asking to be carried and you have a full day of Disney fun ahead of you. No wonder people pretend to be disabled so as to get a wheelchair and whizz to the front of the queue – at least I assume they do. I have been tempted myself, I have to admit.

And once you finally get to the entrance gates it all costs more than seems feasible. It costs so much you are in shock. Not that turning back and going back to the car is an option, seeing as it is a half-hour commute back, and your children have been whipped into a sense of unhealthy anticipation by the merchandising and branding you have been subjected to on the way in – oh yes, you have to pay for it all right. Nor that going on the rides will be an end to the massive cost of it all: wait till you stop for lunch, or get to the souvenir shops at the end of each ride with their expensive cuddly toys and outfits: you will not believe it. And now I am just starting to sound like Victor Meldrew.

At least the kids like it – which is just as well. In fact the truth is the kids adore it: they are enchanted by everything, spellbound when Cinderella serves them a milkshake, overjoyed with the Little Mermaid ride. Disney simply knows how children, the only truly non-grumpy people, tick – it's just that everyone else who takes the children has to put up with it as well. Mysteriously there are some adults who go to Disney without kids, I mean without having kids pressurise you into going, of their own free will, is what I am trying to say, hard though it is to believe.

> *There are some adults who go of their own free will without children to Disneyland. They have got to be mentally ill. You've got to take a good hard look at yourself if for your holiday of choice if you're 40 years of age and you want to walk up and down a comedy pretend street with a giant mouse.*
>
> Stuart Maconie

If the cost of such holidays – both literal and emotional – is not enough to put you off, standing for 45 minutes at a time for a ride that sometimes only lasts a couple of minutes is – face it – sheer insanity, although they tell me that you can now book your slots on rides, which inevitably means that people get there at the crack of dawn, plan a strategic dash round the theme park and book their slots, which will take them a good hour, be hugely competitive and – guess what – probably involve a queue anyway. All this and if you've plumped for the cheaper option, Eurodisney, and it's the wrong time of year, you can factor in rain and wind chill. Nice. Plus in France you might well have to factor in people who don't do queuing, don't get queuing – and now I'm getting all hot and sweaty just thinking about it all. Eurodisney is particularly prone to queue chaos – a glimpse of what it must be like to be an MEP in the canteen at Brussels HQ, I imagine.

> *I found that when you to go to Disneyland in Paris all the ethnic considerations come to the front, so you will be the first person in line and then the gong goes off and all of a sudden there are 187 Germans in front of you and 297 Italians, and you don't know where they came from and you've ended up at the back of the line.*
>
> Jenni Trent Hughes

Course me being British I queue up, you know, religiously, for the two-hour wait for Space Mountain or whatever it is, and the French teenagers are just climbing over the fence endlessly in front of you, just going right in at the front, and no one seems to mind in France. That's what happens: everyone pushes in and I'm standing there exploding with frustration and saying ... tutting almost loudly to try and stop these French people pushing in, and you just don't move at all – that's the experience of Disneyland. You go, 'I think I'll go and stand in a queue for two hours, for two days in fact, and just be uptight and cross because I'm, you know, not able to do what the rest of the Europeans do.'

John O'Farrell

THE RIDES

So how good are these rides, then, which you might waste 45 minutes of your life waiting for? Well, let's see. You could get in a teeny weeny canoe that gets winched up to the top of a ramp and then splash down again in seconds and get wet; or go into a pretend jungle and hear some pretend monkeys in the trees. Or you could queue to get on a ride called It's a Small World, where you get on a little boat like the ones they have in Amsterdam on the canals and go into a sort of underground car park and listen to the song 'It's a Small World After All' sung by midgets over and over and over again and see every country of the world represented by a display of dolls and sleighs and houses – it's all a bit like the Christmas window at Debenham's, but in August. Trouble is the kids adore it, and although my children are now well into their teens, I can still remember that song. It's a song that haunts you: it is depressingly bold and clear, and it has cut a definite ridge in my brain. It will be one of the last things to go as I die; I shall still be able to hear it, even when I am way past remembering my own name or my own whereabouts. That's mean of Disney. Needlessly mean.

Some of the rides that don't throw you about too much are quite sweet, if you have a five-year-old. The Peter Pan ride is quite diverting: you sit on a little umbrella over a model of London by night, there are some Dick Van Dyke-type cockney accents, which if you go round twice you might pick up and find jolly in an ironic sense, but it's over very quickly. Any of the rides which don't make you nauseous or give you an anxiety attack are to be encouraged, since once you are a grumpy old man or a grumpy old woman, chances are you will be anxious about just about everything; when you're middle-aged you're a bit challenged on the courage front, a bit jumpy (actually if you are a grumpy old woman you're a lot jumpy), so you'll be grateful for the rides that are scare free. I have to admit to finding even the Snow White ride a little bit scary; that's one of the toddler rides, but for me there were hints of the ghost train and hints of the wicked witch which were embarrassingly scary.

Sadly once the kids are more than about six they most definitely want scary – demand scary, the scarier the better – and rides that are so dangerous you have to be strapped into them. Suddenly It's a Small World seems oh so wonderful in comparison.

There's always the contemporary Butlins-type idea, like Centre Parcs or Oasis: thousands of people all living on a campus so large you have to hire a bike to get from your lodge to the place where you buy a bottle of milk, all trying to get a badminton court or a slot on the roller rink at once, and if you are unlucky it's raining, and there are thousands of you, all trying to fit their clothes and shoes and mac and rucksack into a locker the size of an A4 file, and then you're all going to be bobbing about together in a pool with a siren or Tarzan effect and a wave machine that sends you knocking into other people. Or you could watch the kids come down the flumes and then queue up for a coffee – lovely. And if you're lucky you come home with a verruca or two. You're so busy packing in all the adventure and fun you can manage in a week that it's one long schedule – must dash over to the other side of the park to get my fencing slot in, or have to dash back to get my swimming stuff to get back to the dome to do my aquafit. It's just like work but more expensive. I challenge anyone not to start looking forward to being back at their desk but maybe that's just grumpy old me.

> *My childhood holiday experiences are almost all tied up with holiday camps with Butlins because I went to Butlins. I've got like a passport stamped with every Butlins in it. If there is some kind of long-service medal for Butlins I am sure I could qualify for it. People sneer at them now but, you know, Centre Parcs are just posh Butlins, aren't they? Just posh Butlins with a glass roof, aren't they?*
>
> Stuart Maconie

Today's version of a holiday camp is a lot of fresh air and exercise. I guess the Butlins holiday was a good deal lazier, involving a lot of time being inert, watching the knobbly-knee competitions, doing the quickstep and being subjected to some very annoying Red Coats.

TEENAGERS

Kids on holiday are exhausting, worrying and high maintenance; they mostly defeat the object of a holiday really. But teenagers are a whole lot worse, because unlike small children, they are there under duress, because you won't let them stay behind and have the house to themselves without you, when what they really want is to turn your house into party HQ for the entire school, and instead you threaten to drag them off to the Pembrokeshire coastal path. Actually, if you are foolish enough to get them to the Pembrokeshire coastal path, utterly fabulous as it is, in my view you had it coming.

And you can't even pull them out of it by bribing them with a Beanie Baby or a go on the rocket launcher on the pavement by the slot machines: not even the longest, most tedious game of Monopoly or Cluedo will pull them round. They pull a holiday face for a full fortnight; they can keep the sneery I-so-wish-I wasn't-your-offspring-I-so-wish-I didn't-have-to-be-here-and-be-with-you sort of face for as long as it takes, in order to persuade you to give in and let them go to the nightclub or bar, or do whatever it is that they want to go off on their own to do.

If they're teenage daughters they're a time bomb waiting to go off: turn your back for a moment and they are being chatted up by the local Don Juan – doesn't seem five minutes since you were building sandcastles for them. Now you're into a whole new set of worries. They look so sumptuous in their skimpy bikinis that waiters start to eye them up.

You might as well leave them at home and let them get on with it. Just bank on buying another house when you get back, but at least you'll have a couple of weeks of peace and quiet.

6
Package Holidays

The trouble with holidays is that it's compulsory to have fun. For non-grumpy people this can mean that they throw themselves (sometimes literally) into making sure they have more fun than seems plausible to you and me, but because on holiday you're not allowed to be grumpy, it makes holidays all the more tricky for the grumpily disposed. For the grumpy fraternity it's hard not to notice – and damn it, we try hard not to notice – that holidays are fraught with hassle, and because the point of them is to make you happy, they often don't. Nothing's perfect enough; nothing's as perfect as you need it to be to be full-on chilled out and fun filled – your bald patch needs sunblock, the pool's been drained for maintenance work and the sun's gone in. The package holiday, which is the nearest most law-abiding citizens will get to a reform centre, is the most challenging of holidays on the cheerful front. It simply involves too many nations, too few king prawns at the buffet and too many other people you don't think you like very much living too close for comfort.

You try to throw yourself into the holiday spirit, you find a gorgeous peaceful idyllic beach away from all the hustle and bustle and soak up the sun, but you can bet your life that whatever you do, whatever lovely little beach you find or bar overlooking the bay, so do half a million other disgruntled holiday makers. Oh, the joys of the package deal! What were you thinking of?

Holiday brochures are now so complicated and so choice-rich that you need a wheelie to get them home from the shop; the summer sun brochure is so complicated and so comprehensive that you need to be a member of Mensa to work it all out. Trouble is you pore over the brochures for a good day and a half, try to agree with your partner on where to go (or how much you want to spend, more like) and then when you get back to the shop and the travel agent – who is either a boy with a silly hairdo who looks as if he has taken part in a wind-tunnel experiment, or a computer-says-no type – you can bet that whatever careful choice you made is full, or doesn't go from Manchester on Fridays unless you fly at three in the morning, or doesn't do single rooms, or the transfer is five hours long. One way or another there is something that you know from bitter past experience you need to avoid that is *un*avoidable. You have wasted a good day cross-referencing holidays and departure dates, only to find you are asking (irritating) travel agent, who seems to be dealing with about four customers at once and spends most of the time on the phone to other travel agents, to find you a holiday that works. You get them to try the bargain ones on the window cards, which obviously don't marry with any of your dates (or anyone else's, evidently) at all or are no longer available. It takes the whole morning, and you still come out with something entirely different from what you went in to book.

Which is why I guess the package deal is dying out. We are simply more capable of doing it ourselves these days – getting cheap deals with the airlines, booking our own car hire, avoiding being lumped in with a coachload of other people. Independent travel is on the up.

Travel agents must suddenly feel like an endangered species. Trouble is doing it yourself on the Internet is not much better: there is so much choice – none of it really either convenient or affordable – that it makes you dizzy. Many of us have tried the independent travel holiday and, liberating as it feels, it comes with four times the hassle of a package. Suddenly a rep would be a welcome sight when you realise that the train you have been waiting for is not running because in Italy it's a bank holiday, and arriving somewhere at 9 p.m. and finding somewhere to stay on spec might well lead to serious disappointment. Maybe this kind of holiday is best left for the young, for the sort of young, fit 20-year-olds who travel with rucksacks that weigh more than they do and are able to sleep rough or on the floor of a booking office – I can't help feeling that the grumpy are over this sort of holiday. Sometimes packages are the only option. But package holidays mean by definition you are doing something en masse, and this is challenging for the grumpy holiday maker.

I am repelled by the idea of package holidays – letting some-one else sort out where you go and where you stay. I was at Luton airport the other day, just wanting to make quite sure that the check-in queue that I was joining was for a flight to Barcelona, and I said to one of the women standing in the queue, 'Is this the flight for Barcelona?' She said, 'I don't know. We're with Horizon holidays.' She didn't know where she was going.

Matthew Parris

THE REP

There she is, clutching the clipboard with the sign on it, in her logo'd neck scarf and her turquoise blouse, looking as if she's had too much to drink and as if she's talking to her mate about how awful the next intake might be – who might have the most losers, the most high-maintenance guests. Liking your guests isn't one of the job criteria, it seems. She's ticking you off and making you feel as if you're on a punitive course. Your fellow holiday makers are gathering by said clipboard; obviously all the shell suits you saw hitting the bar at the airport or being hideously loud on the plane are assembling by the same clipboard as you are – that's a given. She's making out that she's here to help, but everyone knows that her job is clearly to make sure you are going to spend as much money as possible while you are in her care. That's her mission in life. Trouble is she thinks she is a local expert on everything about the place you have just landed in – an assumption based presumably on the fact that she frequents the nightclubs, can speak to the driver in pidgin Spanish and knows where to buy knock-down designer perfume. Big deal.

THE TRANSFER

You were careful not to book a holiday with a flight at 2 a.m. Because you only do that once. Yes, you were really careful, but what you didn't notice was the transfer time from airport to resort, or even if you did notice it and booked the hotel accordingly, you get there and still have the transfer from hell because they're building a 7-lane motorway, which means there's a 30-mile diversion on an unmade road, and so a journey that normally takes 45 minutes takes five hours, on a hair-raising road hugging the cliff edge in an electric storm with your driver smoking and texting simultaneously.

I have reached the end of my tether on some of those when you are on a coach at four in the morning and for some reason I always manage to book the hotel that's the last drop-off and

*you have to go to, like, 45 other hotels, and there's always Mrs
Scroggins who can't find her bag on the coach and then she
discovers that she's left it back at the airport.*

                                                            Jane Moore

*I remember getting on some package holiday thing that was
another disaster. I think we were going to Turkey. Got off this
plane, when they lie to you about how far the apartment is
from the airport and they say it's a couple of hours and this
was actually eleven hours – eleven hours with one nappy. So
that was quite stressful, but what was even more stressful was
the holiday rep had just heard the news that her grandma had
died, and so she was trying to do all this talking to the microphone on the coach, but she was crying all the time, and after
about sort of, you know, 20 miles of this you thought, Well
you're going to have to pull yourself together now, you know,
dead nana or no.*

                                                            Jenny Eclair

*It's not that I am a control freak or anything, I swear, but one
of the reasons I don't like driving in coaches is because you
sometimes have these mad drivers and they are sort of driving
at eight million miles an hour and you are thinking of the
story you heard last summer of the 80 pensioners who came
to an untimely end crashing over the side of a mountain.*

                                                      Jenni Trent Hughes

Of course you can go the other way and get a nice short transfer
time from airport to hotel – say ten minutes – but this just means
your hotel is at the airport, on the runway. So either way you
can't win.

Once everyone is on the coach, and you've waited half an hour
for the inevitable drunks at the bar to find their way to the right

clipboard, the rep gets going and stands at the front of the coach with an unnecessary microphone. She's annoying you already, telling you dazzlingly stupid things about Lanzarote, when clearly what she knows about the island could be written on a Post-it note – one of those really small ones. She's desperate to get back to bed to sleep off last night, and she'll certainly disappear the moment you get to the hotel, when you'll need her most on room allocation.

Of course whenever anything goes wrong and you want to complain you can never find the rep. There's always a sign up; they've always got these desks and you go to the desk and it says the rep will be here between 12 and 10 past 12 on a Thursday in November – never ever available when you want them.

Jane Moore

Holiday reps think that the job is going to be more fun than it actually is. Their whole lives are spoilt by people asking them to do things – it's the complaints they can't really do anything about, you know. I think what usually happens with holiday reps is the newest one, the youngest one, has to deal with the biggest problems, you know, so it's usually some sort of 21-year-old girl and they've just had to drain the pool because some two-year-old, you know, dropped a turd and everyone's going, well, why, why, and she has to … And it's all that sort of thing and I think they have quite a horrible time, actually. I think they can't wait to get home, even if they do live in Sheffield; they're just thinking, Please, please can I get home to Sheffield, where it rains every day but at least there's a Marks and Spencer's.

Jenny Eclair

Everyone knows the whole point of the holiday rep is only to sell you the trips. Get you to spend more money than you need to on trips to the local market or a boat trip round the bay that costs you four times as much as it would if you booked it privately, but you get all-you-can-drink hideous sangria with it, or a three- course sandwich. So her one and only really important mission is to get you along to the welcome meeting, which she sells as something of an induction course – something which might mean that you come home with a full understanding of the history of Lanzarote, assuming there is any – and will allow you to start the holiday by meeting your fellow holiday makers, have a nice free cocktail, that sort of thing. And don't forget that you will need to know the details of going home – this is their last-resort line to get you to come to their wretched meeting.

> *I've been on package holidays but I've always avoided the holiday rep chat. Just don't turn up – you don't have to go. They can't make you, you know; it's not the law that you have to go. They do put the pressure on and you sort of feel, well, I'm duty bound, but no, I can't really listen to somebody younger than me wearing a red Aertex shirt.*
>
> Jenny Eclair

Chirpy chops gets stuck into the welcome meeting spiel, and it's worse than going to a pantomime. She's got the big sell down to a T. On and on she drones; your holiday's ebbing away, the sun's going in and you might as well be back in the office with the flip charts and pointy pens and presentation. She's telling you all the things you don't need to know; she's doing the big sell on a stupid Spanish night out for about 40 quid a pop. We've all fallen for the kind of trips on offer: the overland safari to the Pyramids, which is supposed to take three hours but you know will take 13; the whale watching with no whales; the Jolly Pirate cruise with drunken hooligans hurling themselves off the boat, or worse hurling you off the boat; appalling-to-the-point-of-embarrassing traditional belly dancing nights with belly dancers from Slough; trips to hideously dull bird parks in what they laughingly call the rainforest, which is really just a wood with a café in the middle; trips that take all day and involve a lot of waiting around for other people to catch up or sitting in hot coaches all day. They're all the kind of thing you could have done without, eating into your relaxation time, me time, time with no deadlines, no hassle and no pressure, oh, and no other people. There's a clue to getting holidays right: keep exposure to other holiday makers to a minimum.

Inevitably with package deals there is going to be a lot of pushing and shoving. Truth is you are never going to see the people who are on the same holiday as you again, but effectively it is the survival of the fittest, because guess what: there are only three tables overlooking the beach, only two sun umbrellas by the pool and only ten rooms overlooking the sea, and once you know there's a great table with a sea view, and you're sitting at the one by the loos, you want the one by the sea; and once you notice that there is a nice wing of the hotel overlooking the bay, and your room is by the air-conditioning vent, you have no choice but to join in the competition to get what is on offer and get as much of it as possible. In short, you have signed up for undignified scrum and stress from morning till night.

There are unwritten and illogical rules which apply to holiday bagsings, such as this is our table because we bagsied it on the first night, or this is our patch on the beach because we've pitched our windbreak and spread all our possessions over a patch the size of a football pitch, or this is our seat on the coach because we grabbed it on day one and we are simply not letting go of it.

You tend to have the same seat on a coach and if you try to move to a different seat once you have sat down then every-body gets incredibly cross, because this is the sheep mentality: you know, you're being escorted, you are on a coach trip, you are being looked after; you haven't had the gumption to book anything on your own, you are being taken into the centre of Paris from your grotty hotel in a group of people, so to do any-thing that is out of the ordinary like move across the aisle causes absolute mayhem.

Nina Myskow

Naturally, the pool area is going to be the most stressful and the one with the most pushing and shoving. Don't think lolling by the pool is going to be a doddle: 500 guests and only 100 sun-loungers to go round is a recipe for international incidents for the week ahead. You can't just go and sprawl on a lounger when the mood takes you for some reason; you have to be in possession of it all day. And if you're stupid enough to have a lie-in you've had it – missed the boat: by 8.30 a.m. all the other clever-clog nations have already set up base camp and bagsied the lot. When we were filming for *Grumpy Old Holidays* in Tenerife the hotel where we were filming stacked their loungers up last thing at night and chainlocked them together to prevent bagsying till 7.30 a.m., and from 7.15 a.m. onwards there would be a queue forming by the sun-loungers. So to be in the queue to get your lounger out and into the spot you liked for the day meant you actually had to set your alarm. You might just as well have been at home and at work for all the relaxation and spontaneity your holiday was giving you.

Of course on day one you sleep in and hope that sun-lounger war is not in evidence. Then you spend the rest of the day sitting on the floor next to the dustbins, so you don't do that again. By day two usually you notice that one side of the pool area is shaded after 2 p.m. and so now you not only have to get three sun-loungers but have to get them on the right side of the pool. Then you notice how few sunshades there are, and it all becomes a huge worry, and you are only one step away from taking it in turns to eat breakfast while the other one holds on to territory gained.

The Germans are – as we know – expert at the bagsying sun-lounger war, but the Russians are overtaking them, in my experience, in terms of sheer cheek and laziness. Last time we went to the sea the Russians were there in great numbers and would bagsy a line of loungers for the morning by the pool and then another line of them for the afternoon on the beach, monopolising at least 12 per family of four. Bagsied, I might add, with the bathroom flannel – they couldn't even be bothered to find a book or a sarong to add authenticity and weight to territory gained, and not even the bathroom towel or robe but just the bathroom flannel. I took them off and threw them on the beach in anger, a sort of beach vigilante. Wonder I didn't end up in hospital.

You've told yourself you were above bagsying the sun-loungers – you don't even want to lie on them that much; but if other people want them, then you want them. If there's a best spot, you want it. Suddenly it's if you can't beat them, join them. So you're up at dawn staking your claim, doing some heavy construction work marking out your territory: rolling huge concrete-based umbrellas that the Russians had yesterday round the pool, and, when you realise you might have slept in ten minutes too long, might have left it too late, doing that walk which is really a run but is supposed to convince people you are still walking. No, truth is you're in it to win it, as they say. You'll do anything to hang on to your loungers and sun umbrella and keep them out of enemy hands; you'll stop at nothing. Pity they don't sell land mines at reception.

I think they should have timers on, and if no one is lying on

...and this is
when we captured
the sunlounger from
the Russians
at dawn...

the loungers when the alarm goes off they should automatically be handed over to behind enemy lines. God forbid someone should fall asleep at the café or leave their post for a moment. There's probably a political manifesto in that.

There is this rather old-fashioned racist cliché that the Germans put their towels on the sun-loungers and grab the best spots, and it's true, they do. They go there and you think, I can't believe this – it's like a Bob Monkhouse joke, you know, that I'm living through; but they really do in places I've been to, like sort of Tunisia or Spain. You get there and there's all these towels laid out and, you know, territory has been occupied, and you can't do anything about it; you can't, you know, remove them, you

If you think the Russians' sun-lounger habits are bad, maybe you should avoid hiring a car with them.

Russians are Europe's worst drivers, with 25 per cent admitting to having had sex behind the wheel, according to a new survey. They also found that Russians drive without using seatbelts, break speed limits, drive through red lights and drive drunk.

36 per cent of Russian drivers admit to regularly exceeding speed limits – the highest rate in Europe.

daren't sort of take the towels off – that would be far too sort of pushy for a British person. So you end up just huddled in the corner next to the drains whilst they're all sort of doing acrobatics in the pool and scaring the kids.

John O'Farrell

I think the Germans, they get a bad press. I've got nothing against the Germans and I think if they get there first, good for them. If you wanted it, you should have got up earlier and got there.

Don Warrington

I mean, we do know – obviously history has taught us – that they have got fairly shall we say expansive attitudes, the Germans, they're always keen to move into other countries and sort of colonise them for longer or shorter periods as the rest of the world lets them; but I don't know if they're as bad as people make them out, really. I mean, I'm always a bit loath to start saying, 'Oh, aren't the Germans abroad terrible?' because the British abroad are hardly P.G. Woodhouse, are they? You know what I mean – no, we're not all Stephen Fry,

Germans take their holidays seriously. Stressed German men are taking lessons in order to learn how to have fun on holiday. Courses have been set up in which uptight blokes are taught how to build sandcastles, apply sun lotion, dance and dress casually.

The courses were established after a survey revealed that German women are fed up with husbands who cannot relax on holiday. Wives complained that their hubbies insisted on walking around resorts with personal organisers and constantly phoned work.

At the course HQ in Düsseldorf there is a huge sandpit in which the men can practise having fun.

looking at quaint local churches and making bon mots. We're usually there sort of vomiting, aren't we, and attacking the local people.

Stuart Maconie

If you're Michael Winner, though, the answer is simply to demand that the staff do your sun-lounger bagsying for you; get them to sort it out, tackle the Germans – demand, what's more, that your sun-lounger is basically a single bed with a mattress on it and a gorgeous shade to keep you cool. Give them hell; scare the living daylights out of everyone. Now how hard can that be? But it's no good pretending we are above sun-lounger war. We are so not above sun-lounger war.

It was one of those all-inclusive holidays, so you are on a compound, but our bungalow was actually slightly off the compound in a sort of cul-de-sac a little bit away. We had a special key to get in, but the key didn't work until nine o'clock in the

*morning, so to bagsy the sun-lounger I had to throw myself,
hurtle à la Fosby Flop over the electric fence and run to the
place where you got the sun-lounger.*

Jenny Eclair

Sometimes it's hard not to wonder why you don't just stay at
home and lie in your back garden.

*I mean, it's interesting about the Germans, because they do
nab a lot of the sun-loungers, but actually when you think
about it they are just incredibly organised. Because I've got a
toddler, I'm always up at 4 a.m. anyway, so I've become one of
those if-you-can't-beat-them-join-them people and I am
obsessed. I will be, right, it's 4 a.m., off I go with the towel,
spreading it out across four sun-loungers, you know, and this
that and the other, and I tie sarongs on to the corner just for
extra possession.*

Jane Moore

If you like making friends on holiday, like chatting to strangers
round the pool, and like exchanging addresses at the end and
being on one another's Christmas card list, then chances are you
like the sociability of package deals. But then again, if that's the
case chances are you probably won't have bought this book.

Family tension is probably tough enough for most of us, even
on holiday, without the added factor of being fed up because
the people you chummed up with from Solihull only bought
one round last night and the night before that too, come to
think of it.

*I don't like package holidays. I don't want to go somewhere
with a bunch of people who I don't know and probably don't
like. I'm not very social; I'm not very good at, you know, joining in. I suppose the worst thing about it is that you're duty
bound to have a good time and people keep asking you how*

you are and I don't like that – don't want them to ask me how
I am, and so no, package holidays are not ... I don't under-
stand them anyway. What does it mean, a package holiday?

Don Warrington

Joining in – ah yes, grumpy people are not good at joining in, and
this makes package holidays and such a challenging amount of
other people together in one place *challenging*.

My son and I went off to Turkey, which is a place I have been
to 17 times, so I thought, you know, you can't go wrong with
Turkey. I ended up in a hotel, and no disrespect to anyone
intended, but when the grannies have tattoos it's just not the
place for me. So I would sit by the pool, and every night there
was a fight because Kevin junior slapped some other kid, and
then the fathers got involved, and you would get up in the
morning and there would be people with pints and it would be
ten o'clock in the morning. Not good.

Jenni Trent Hughes

No, truth is that, like it or not, for the truly grumpy person, hell
is other people on a package holiday, and when you go on packages, other people are everywhere.

The idea of being kind of herded ... I think you become like a
sheep, you know. The fact that they think you can't organise
your own transport from the hotel to the airport or vice versa,
you know: you've got to be kind of gathered together, and
you're always waiting for somebody, you're always waiting
for some dickhead whose, you know, whose alarm clock
hasn't gone off.

Nina Myskow

Oh what jolly fun it all sounds ... not.

1

Men and Women on Holiday

As a couple, you see more of one another on holiday than you do at home – more even than you do at Christmas, since at Christmas you have sprouts to peel and black bags to fill with rubbish as excuses to get away from one another. If you've only been together for less than six months, chances are it's on holiday that you'll notice he leaves the top off the toothpaste, or that she is a bit of a fusspot about the pillows on her side of the bed, or that when they say they'll be ready in 15 minutes it means 45, in which case a holiday is often make or break relationship-wise. Conversely, if you've been together for a long time, the differences are well and truly in evidence on holiday and harder to ignore. And to think you paid a lot of money to subject yourselves to this. You're thrown together 24/7, which is good – ish – , but guess what, even on holiday women carry on being women and men carry on being men, so even on holiday tragically domestic bliss continues to elude most of us. I say most of us because I suspect that if you've been together for more than a couple of years, or if you're shall we say mature, then you've

Do you really think the burglars will give a damn if the place is a bit untidy?

come to the conclusion that domestic bliss is something that happens only in *The Sound of Music*, in that scene where they all go off for the picnic, and even then if you think about it she was a governess, not their mother, and someone else had packed the sandwiches.

First of all, truth is your partner will probably be different to you in some very significant ways in holiday terms. He might be in charge of people at work, you might have made him think from time to time that he is in charge of (some) things at home, but either way, once you leave home to go on holiday there is some sort of power struggle brewing. One partner is usually in charge of worrying. Whichever partner is the worrier will ask so many times if the tickets are here, or the currency sorted or the visa got or the pick-up time checked, that the other partner mentally gives over responsibility for it. And tragically the chances of the not worrying partner actually forgetting to do a lot of the things they said they would are high because they are nagged about it so much.

In my experience, women get tetchy to the point of almost as bad as the run-up to Christmas before they go on holiday. A woman will have sorted out three wardrobes and have the clothes washed, ironed and in piles ready to go in the case; she will have packed the medication; if they're taking kids chances are she will have thought things through in some detail – colouring books, iPods, sweets and face wipes for the journey, nappies for the transfer, nappy bags, books for the kids, surprise presents for really bad long journeys; she will have put all the plants in the bath and watered them, told Marjorie next door where they're going and asked her to pop round every other day; and she will have had to sort out her own mother's hospital appointment for when she is away.

I suppose you can only draw from your own experience. In effect, in our house, I do all the home bits and he does all the travel bits. Trouble is because I am a control freak I really want to keep an eye on both areas of responsibility – I want to have a foot in both camps. Experience tells me that because he is busy with big day job, little details like booking interconnecting rooms, or pre-booking plane seats, or checking how far the car park is from the airport, will slip through the net or fall off the end of his list of things to do. Little things like how long it takes to get in the silly shuttle bus from the hotel car park to the terminal, or which terminal we are going to, or taking the travel insurance details with him. Stuff like that. He will have been busy deciding which novels are to go in, and buying the best guidebooks for castles, ruins and typical rustic restaurants, while I have been busy stocking up on Imodium and Wet Wipes. Then there's all the admin that has to get done before a fortnight away – bills to be paid, phone calls to be made: maddeningly time consuming and all making you more stressed out and bad tempered than normal. Result: foul mood, tetchy, jumpy, blotchy and screamy build-up to leaving the house.

For some couples, it's then the inevitable really big punch-up happens. What time are you actually going to set off? He says about an hour before she thinks they all need to leave; she wants to hoover herself out the house, she wants to make the beds properly, plump cushions, empty dishwasher and sweep kitchen floor, because she doesn't want to come back to mess (which to the grumpy woman would negate all benefit from taking the holiday in the first place) and conversely, in fact tragically, it will add to her enjoyment of the holiday if the house is properly tidy and clean for when she comes back. He can't see the point of worrying about what the house is going to look like when no one is going to be in it.

Even when you set off it goes on, the gender conflict: when to leave the departure lounge for the gate, when to start boarding – all these things are the sort of things which eke out any differences between couples and often are gender related. Then there's the loo crisis, which happens to women when they go on a plane – or is it just me? I don't much like having to go to the loo on the plane itself; I assume that once I get in there and lock the door it is going to crash, as in that film *Castaway* when Tom Hanks has done just that – gone to the loo and locked the door – and the plane explodes in mid-air; I assume that once I go to the loo something catastrophic is going to happen. I don't even like leaving my seat much, but of course the moment you think you won't be able to go to the loo, you badly want the loo, so in my case there is a lot of going before I get on, and then going again. In fact, thinking about it, the loo crisis lasts for most of the holiday full stop. Will there be a loo, what will the loo be like and when will we get to it? Men, or the men I know, seem to be simply oblivious.

There's not a single thing that I am not worrying about at all times, so all there is for me on holiday is just the same anxiety but upped about 100 notches, whereas my husband, who's the only man I go on holiday with these days, will relax, yeah, and that's not really something I can do on holiday.

Arabella Weir

Maddeningly men seem to be able to switch off on holiday so much more quickly than women. Men seem to manage to get stuck in to a fat novel the moment they are on the plane, irrespective of having toddlers or teenagers travelling with them, while women are by then so relieved to have left the ground and left their to-do-before-we-go-on-holiday lists behind that they stare out of the window, just enjoying a little bit of inertia in between fishing things out of the travel bag on the floor for everyone else.

Not that it stops when you get there: still women find it harder to download, debrief and chill out. There are so many other things that get in the way.

There are two distinct types of holiday, which for the gender issue make a big division: hotel or self-catering. And it is when you arrive at the self-catering option that the gender differences really come into their own. Suddenly you realise that you have brought all your daily domestic squabbles with you, but this time, to add to the misery, the house doesn't have a proper cooker.

I think men are able to go, 'I'm on holiday, goodness me, that's it' – the abdication of responsibility is complete and utter. Where's the cold beer? With the beer and the fat paperback, quite quickly. And you'll four or five hours later still be sort of going through the saucepan arrangements in the kitchen and saying, 'Yes, well, but I haven't got a pie dish,' and there's, 'Come out, the weather's lovely, you know, come outside, have a beer, we're on holiday for Christ's sake,' and you're like, 'No, no, no, really, I need you to know there's one tog duvet on the

spare bed and it's just not going to work and let's speak to the
rep.' I mean, you know, you effectively transplant your roles in
real life into the holiday situation.

Kathryn Flett

Once you've unpacked the crumpled tangled mess that was the
things you ironed and put them in the wardrobe, assuming you
could find enough coat hangers (which you won't have), what
everyone really wants to do is relax and start the holiday. The
moment you've got to your destination and changed your room,
the holiday clock is ticking. You need to get out there, by the pool
and start having fun – and of course that is a pressure in itself.

It's often tragically the case that women and men like doing
different things on holiday. Women, as we all know, like lolling;
they like getting themselves nicely set up on a sun-lounger with
some Steely Dan on their iPod, a nice cool drink and some peace
and quiet, with the thrill of a market full of bargains and nice
cheap leather shoes in the afternoon and then a romantic supper
overlooking a sunset of an evening. Where's the hard in that?
Whereas on the whole men like looking at castles and ruins, and
those romantic suppers that women dream of probably happen
only on the poster advertising the restaurant in the lift, and even
in the specially posed photo they look as if they don't mean it.

There's a very basic difference between men and women and
what they want on holiday. Women want to lie in the sun-
shine; men don't. They always get bored after five minutes;
they always, you know, pace up and down the beach, saying,
'I'm going to the shops' or 'I am going to paddle, I'm going to
the blah blah' – they will not lie down, they just don't like to
lie down. And the other thing: they don't put suntan lotion on,
which drives you wild anyway.

Nina Myskow

Well, women genuinely want to go and relax and get a little bit of a tan, and they sort of have a vision of themselves feeling carefree, they sort of have a snapshot in their heads of sort of what it must feel like to be a little bit thinner and a little bit lighter and maybe on the beach sort of reaching up for a beach ball in a sort of balletic move.

Jenny Eclair

Some men do like a bit of lolling. Michael Winner, for instance, has turned it into an art form.

Women like a lot of treatment. They love treatment, they love massage, they love hot coals being thrown at them, they love people walking on their bottoms with bare feet, you know. Well, that doesn't worry me: they can go and have the treatments. I'll stay looking at the sea.

Michael Winner

HOLIDAY ROWS

Even honeymoons are not devoid of conflict between the sexes – actually especially honeymoons. You've invested so much in the honeymoon, and those special honeymoon hotels must be terrifying – all that pressure to be in love, look in love, act in love all

---

The day for a blazing row

It's a bad time for divorce after the August bank holiday and Christmas. But September is also the time when families have been together and are disappointed with the family holiday.

The most common arguments are reportedly those over money, sex, work, children and housework.

the time. I'll bet that most of them are bickering after a week of all that high-octane romance. Probably finish the partnership off before you even get home. After all, suddenly you can't just decide to part ways at the airport when you get home. Well, you could, but it would be a bit careless remaining married for only a fortnight – think of all the presents you'd have to send back. Holidays are like that – they throw you together in a way that is either intensely fabulous or intensely annoying, or a mixture of both – but on honeymoon everything is supposed to be perfect, so when a honeymoon's disappointing you are definitely in top-of-the-range grumpy territory.

I remember we were so looking forward to our honeymoon because it was two weeks, us on our own, and we went to Mauritius and it rained for the first nine days so, you know, everyone was like, 'Oh, but you have your love to keep you warm...' Day three massive argument, opposite ends of the beach.

Jane Moore

Cockneys top hols cheats

It's been said that Cockney lads are the worst love cheats in the country: in a survey many said they would cheat on their girlfriend if abroad. This was a dismal show of commitment compared to monogamous Scots, who were the least likely to cheat.

Girls from London were also the most likely to cheat on boyfriends.

Research has revealed that faithfulness depends upon where you live. Holidaymakers from Glasgow are said to be the most committed to their partners.

Women were far less likely to cheat than men, with a huge amount of men admitting to cheating whilst abroad compared to only a handful of women.

Get away! Hol tiffs abound

Research has found that one in three British couples have a huge row on holiday. Most big bust-ups happen in the first two days, before partners relax and recover from the preparations. And many of those who argue are people under most strain from work or relationships.

Some feel like their break hasn't started until about day three of a trip. Many felt stressed by finding the right location, getting to the airport and worrying over arrangements.

Counsellors and psychotherapists have found that travel itself may be stressful but more important is our difficulty in making the transition from work to play. For about two days you can feel irritable, disorientated and ill at ease until you have settled into your new holiday environment.

HOLIDAY ROMANCES

Of course you might meet someone while you're away and go in for a holiday romance, which is exciting, I imagine. Trouble is meeting someone by the side of the pool or in a nightclub can be fun, but without being able to put them into a normal everyday context, so to speak, you might go horribly wrong, and let's face it if they're working there for the season, or they're a local, chances are they are on a fortnightly loop of romance.

So you're best to be warned.

Holiday romances over in a week

Those looking for long-lasting love on holiday are in for a disappointment, surveys have shown. Almost nine in ten holiday romances are over in a week, with flings lasting only few days on average.

Both men and women have admitted that a mix of sun, sand and sangria made it easier to fall in love. Some women found tight trunks and thongs on men are a turn-off. They also disliked chunky jewellery, open-toed sandals, knotted handkerchiefs on heads and string vests. Male pet hates included underarm hair on women, ill-fitting bikinis and fake designer wear. But almost half of men and women said they could find people attractive on holiday whom they would not fancy back home.

I think holiday romances are pretty doomed as a rule, aren't they? Cos of course what you fall in love with is the very holidayness of it all. I mean, you know, he's not farting and going to work in a stinking vest and going 'Don't know what time I'll be home,' and it's not raining and it's all sunny and gorgeous, and he probably looks all right in his Speedos. I mean, there's your pointer for a starter: you should never get off with a man wearing Speedos.

Arabella Weir

I was quite keen on someone and then I – I made a sort of surprise visit back and he had absolutely no idea who I was. He must have literally ripped through every foreigner in this resort, so I mean, I was just like one in a million kind of

Swedish, Italian, Dutch girls that he'd helped himself to, and of course I thought I was special in some way. Hi, I'm here. Sorry, who are you?

Arabella Weir

Grumpy or not grumpy, the truth is that girls are girls on holiday and boys are boys, and sometimes that can work for a happy hour or two, it has to be said. Well, in retrospect it does anyway.

8

The Beach

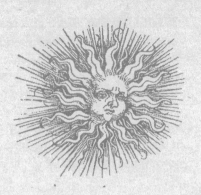

For grumpy people beaches are often the biggest let-down of all. Because on a beach you think you are going to have the time of your life. Even the word 'beach' conjures up the ultimate feeling of carefree, happy-go-lucky fun; you think by going to the beach you ought – surely – to have a wonderful time. But if you're grumpy, often you don't.

Unfortunately, once again your memory has played tricks on you. You remember idyllic days on the beach as a small child, carrying a bucket of water from the sea to a moat in the sandcastle your dad helped you make for hours on end, and prodding crabs in a rock pool to your heart's content. You had all the time in the world, your mum had packed some ham sandwiches, your parents were in a good mood and you paddled until it started to get dark. You didn't notice the sewage outlet, or the hideous white-trash caravan-park fraternity letting their dogs foul all over the sand dunes – your radar didn't pick up any of those annoying things at all. Then when you're a teenager you frolicked on a beach, you ran in and out of the water with your friends, you showed off your body with gay abandon, you snogged, you fell in love, you got drunk, you did mad things like building barbecues at midnight, you played Frisbee, you were carefree. But when you're older, and grumpier, and the radar is finely tuned to pick up all manner of irritations, on a beach, as with New Year's Eve, you think you are going to have a wonderful time, but the reality is disappointing; you think that the beach is going to make you feel as you did when you were on beaches when you were young, but alas beaches let you down.

I like a beach, normally, until I get on one, and then I notice all the things that are irritating about it.

You have this idyllic memory of your childhood of this, you know, lovely beach where you made a dam from the stream coming down the beach and you go back there as an adult and you realise that the stream is actually a sewage outlet and there's, you know, bits of dubious tissue paper coming down and your children are saying, 'Oh look I've found a little polythene parachute,' and you're going, 'Right, I think we won't play here, children,' and that is the journey from childhood to adulthood, that stream – realising actually what's in it.

John O'Farrell

When you booked the holiday you were told that the beach was a stone's throw away, but you get there and realise that the stone would have to be thrown by an Olympic shot putter. Or more likely you'll have to get there every day by shuttle bus. So the first problem is that when you head for the beach you have to remember everything you are going to need on the beach all day. And because enjoying yourself, being happy and being ungrumpy is hard work, there is a lot to remember for a day's frolicking on the beach: sunblock, sunglasses, reading sunglasses, the current novel, another novel in case the current novel turns out to be crap, a hat, a drink, lipsil, a camera and so it goes on. Of course

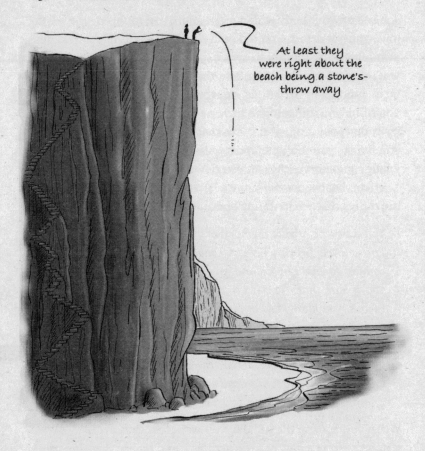

At least they were right about the beach being a stone's-throw away

all these things are key to your enjoyment of the day on the beach and inevitably you will forget the very thing you wanted the most, such as your pen or your iPod, and then you'll have to spend the day without it, feeling grumpy, or bite the bullet and trudge back in the sweltering heat to the hotel again.

Then there's so much to worry about on a beach, especially if you have kids: jellyfish, sharks, rip tides, broken glass, muggers, oil, effluence, raw sewage and – last but not least – the lack of loos. Yes, OK, there are sand dunes, or there is the sea itself to use in an emergency, but it might not be – how shall we put it? – that sort of emergency, and then you're into major hike to loo or café with loo. More pressure, more worry.

Yes, the idea of the beach is appealing until you get there. Then you remember how annoying beaches really are. You forgot how much sand there is on a beach, getting in your shoes and sandwiches, sticking to your sunblock, making you itchy and irritable – it's everywhere. It might be so hot you can't stand on it without scalding the bottom of your feet. And it scratches …I can still remember my mother brushing the sand off my still-wet feet to get my shoes and socks on at the end of a windy day on the beach, and sand, I remember very well, can be a scratchy, spiteful substance that sticks to you like glue. Even rinsing one foot and then balancing on the other doesn't work: you end up with a foot full of sand every time. It gets in your ears, in your hair and of course in your eyes.

The worst thing about trying to relax on holiday is that everything has to be perfect for the relaxation to really sort of take over. So you get down to the beach and you've got to bagsy somewhere that's got some shade but not too much shade – so you'll find your perfect spot and you'll put your towel down. I don't really like sand because, you know, once it gets wet sand is cement basically, that's what it is, that is the chemical compound of sand and water: it is cement. You get it in your bottoms – that is all I'm going to say. So you've got your towel down and you are lying there and OK, we're starting to dry, put your hand out, like that, and on the one side you've got the rotting corpse of a dead rat and the other side you've got a pant liner. It's hard to relax on a beach, I find.

Jenny Eclair

Most beach users view shark attack as the most threatening risk to their lives. It is estimated that there are up to 75 shark attacks each year worldwide, with up to 10 resulting in death. Most recorded shark attacks occur in near-shore areas because this is the area most frequented by humans.

Nice. South Africa is particularly dodgy, shark attack-wise, so if you are reading this book on the plane to a holiday in Cape Town I am sorry. At one beach a shark shield was set up to try to cut down fatal shark attacks. The nets were implemented because in 1957 five people were killed in the area by sharks in a span of 100 days.

Then there's the jellyfish to worry about. These range from a couple of inches to three feet in diameter. The sea wasp is the most dangerous: each year it kills at least two people and seriously injures many more. It contains up to 500 feet of tentacles with an extremely potent and fast-acting venom that is able to stop an adult human's heart within three minutes. So that's going to enhance your swimming in Australia, where you get them, nicely, I'd say.

I increasingly like the sort of beach that is raked and tidied and dusted every morning (which defeats the point really – you might as well just sit by the pool or on your balcony). I like a manicured beach, with a low risk of broken glass and nub ends, but manicured beaches are expensive and mean beach attendants, and beach attendants are a hideous pond life form: medallion men who run a patch of beach and charge the earth for a scrappy sun-lounger and sunshade and earn so much money from it all winter, presumably, in Barbados and have nothing much to do all day but take your money and eye up prettier and slimmer women than you. I think it's called the Italian Riviera. Then

- The most poisonous jellyfish is the Australian sea wasp, or box jellyfish, with enough venom to kill 60 people.
- The largest jellyfish ever found was a lion's mane, with a bell 2 metres across and tentacles extending more than 35 metres.
- The notorious Portuguese man-of-war is not a jellyfish at all but a collection of different organisms including stinging tentacles.
- Jellyfish have both male and female characteristics. One group releases sperm and the other eggs that mix in the water.
- A collection of jellyfish is known as a smack.

everything that is on the beach or near the beach is at a premium. People charge a fortune, or forbid you to use their loos unless you buy lunch – endless rules and regulations, which mean that one way or another you have to pay through the nose for any level of comfort at all.

And the awful truth is that get to a certain age and you do need a sun-lounger: lying on a beach towel on a beach is utterly uncomfortable. When I was a teenager, I think, I would loll about on a beach towel and be relatively happy, but now I am deeply uncomfortable sitting or lying on anything other than what is effectively a double mattress. I get all stiff and I can't get up without going on all fours, which is humiliating. Consequently the whole thing is much more expensive. Some people stay at hotels that are so gobsmackingly expensive and luxurious that they virtually move your bed out on to the beach every day for you. Now that's sounding more like it...

Not only do you have to have a sun-lounger on a beach but it has to be a good class of sun-lounger, and it has to have a very big mattress. You know what, you're lying on this thing nearly all day, you know, so it's very important that you're comfortable on a beach, cos they're not comfortable places, beaches. You put a towel down on a beach – very uncomfortable.

Michael Winner

Getting yourself comfortable and settled on a beach is a very serious business.

You're recommended whatever beach, in whatever island, and you get there, and instantly there are several things you need to check out. The consistency of the sand, is it gravelly sand, is it sandy sand, is it hot, is it going to burn your feet if you take your flip-flops off? How far is it from the car to the desirable sun-lounger? You know, did you bring enough x, y or z to cover all eventualities? How far is it from the sun-lounger to the bar to eat the junk food? Is it such a posh beach that there's waiter service and they'll come and charge you a zillion quid to bring you your thing with the umbrella in it? Do you actually have to be next to the stunningly beautiful Italian girl on the next sun-lounger that your partner's sort of trying not to ogle from behind us?

Kathryn Flett

Then again if it's pebbly, try getting comfy at all without a proper mattressed sunbed – impossible. And try to get in the sea on a pebbly beach – impossible without an old pair of trainers, in my experience, but a marvellous show for everyone watching people trying their best to walk in over the pebbles without screaming out in pain.

There is nothing worse than a pebbled beach. Why do you want to lie on a pebbled beach? You know, it's just stupid: a road is more comfortable than a pebbled beach. I don't like a black beach; sometimes you can go to those places and can't remember that where they're volcanic, that's black sand. Ooh, there's nothing worse – it's like spending two weeks face down in an ashtray.

Jenny Eclair

The beach is like broken glass and pebbles and this wind would, you know … Pebbledash, essentially, you all day kind of exfoliate yourself with these shards of masonry.

Stuart Maconie

OK, some beaches are – I imagine – physically perfect, or perfect enough. You can probably get settled down on an exclusive Caribbean turquoise beach, and have it to yourself, and there's a loo, and there's a nice gentle surf and a sun-lounger and somewhere nice for lunch; but all those things are almost certainly never going to happen simultaneously unless you are Richard Branson and own your own island. It's all a bit like finding out Father Christmas doesn't really exist.

I mean, it's incredibly stressful. I don't know how anyone enjoys it. The only way round it, of course, is to have your own beach. It all comes back to hurling money at the problem, really.

Kathryn Flett

SUNBATHING

Go on a beach-type holiday and you've got to come home with some sort of tan. It's no good looking as pale as you were when you went away or no one will believe you went away at all. But tans don't come easily. Juggling factor 30, factor 15 and pre-salon after sun – there's not a minute's peace. Day one you've got to do ten minutes on your front and 15 on your back, then swap the factor 20 and roll over. You're like a basting chicken on a spit and about as uncomfortable. And still you burn your bald patch, overdo it, get prickly heat and ruin your holiday some more. Even sunbathing isn't easy.

> *I love sunbathing. I dream about sunbathing. I plan it. I spend a fortune going to find it. But when I am actually there and I'm lying there, I think, my God, I am bored and three minutes have passed.*
>
> Nina Myskow

Sunbathing has got so much more complicated, so expensive and now of course so damn dangerous. When I was a kid we used to dowse ourselves in olive oil and vinegar; no one had heard of sunblock, so sunburn was a regular feature of summer holidays and with all that oil and vinegar presumably everyone was smelling as if they worked in the local chip shop.

EXPOSING YOUR BODY

All these things make being on a beach infinitely tricky and don't necessarily lead to the much-needed idle relaxation and serious chilling out. But this stress and anxiety pales in comparison to the real stress of being on a beach, which is that being on holiday in the sun means you need to expose some of your middle-aged body – hence the popularity, presumably, of holidays in Iceland. It's more stressful than you'd bargained for, given the dreaded midriff bulge, and for women of a certain age it can be very trying – but not as trying as it is for the men they are sitting next to.

> *You know where you are in the pecking order. You very, very quickly ascertain that, you know … It's supremely good shuffling the deck of cards and putting them in their … knowing…*

good God, look at that stomach, two loungers up, but thank
God for the lardo three loungers down that way. So you're
pretty much guaranteed to never be the best or the worst, real-
ly; you're just going to be kind of average, and thank the Lord
for that.

Kathryn Flett

It's the am-I-as-fat-as-her? game, or show-me-someone-who's-
the-same size-as-I-am game, which women can't help themselves
playing on a beach. Very, very tricky for men indeed.

I always know I'm the fattest person around the pool or on the
beach. Even if my eyes tell me that's not true, I always feel I am
if not the fattest then the flabbiest, and there's just no way
round that. I mean, I look at other fat women and instead of
feeling a kind of sisterhood, I kind of despise them, because
they remind me of what I am, so it is not really very happy, is
it? Why I spend all this money to go and do that I don't know.
It's a kind of torture.

Nina Myskow

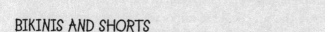

BIKINIS AND SHORTS

To make matters worse, when you say the word 'holiday' men
hear the word 'bikini'. Watching young lovelies in luscious little
teeny weeny numbers is a nice spectator sport on the beach, if
they can sneak a look without anyone seeing. Women of a certain
age would prefer age-segregated beaches; once they reach middle age, obviously they have hidden beauty and elegance, but
perhaps bikinis are best avoided.

There is a day when basically you look at your legs and you
think, well, that is cellulite. Cellulite is God's message to say
it's time to stop wearing a bikini. I mean, the thing is, what I

don't understand is why nobody has designed a swimsuit that covers the biggest problem for the middle-aged woman which is the upper arm problem. So I am thinking long-sleeved swimming costume, a light fabric, you know, but a long-sleeved, or maybe just a three-quarter sleeve, cos they are quite elegant – maybe a bit of a polo neck as well.

Jenny Eclair

These days I am in a costume. I have had my bikini days and I think there's something about bikinis on the over-forties … It's tricky. Maybe it's the bikinis; maybe it's because I'm too tight to spend £500 on a Liz Hurley bikini. I don't see the point of spending that much money on something so small. I'd rather spend 25 quid in M&S and have something big that covers me, you know. That's value for money, really, isn't it?

Kathryn Flett

Enter the sarong, designed with a mother of two teenage daughters in mind. I keep my sarong on at all times, unless I am lying down and the flabby bits flatten out a teeny weeny bit. The sarong is marvellous – even keep it on in the water, I say. And we women, being the practical creatures we are, and probably ex-girl guides, are marvellously inventive with our sarongs.

A sarong is an absolutely invaluable garment. I mean, it is a piece of cloth basically and I have had mine probably since about the end of the 1980s, and it has been invaluable because not only does it hide the thighs but you can use it as, you know, if you have to do any ironing – sometimes they don't give you an ironing board in a hotel – and when you're on a weird holiday, you can use it because you can't iron on carpet, that doesn't work, so you put that down, you can use it to flap mosquitoes away, and you can use it as a tablecloth.

Nina Myskow

Not that the fashion crisis on holiday begins and ends with the bathers, because it might be hot and it might be humid, and then shorts are a tempting option, but of course for the grumpy old woman on holiday unless you are a size 10 shorts are perhaps best left on the shelf. Why do you think they don't do them in your size?

> *I think that a lot of women fall into the trap of the practical khaki shorts and they think, well, you know, it's kind of efficient. It's not really, cos you go around looking like Captain Mainwaring from Dad's Army, which is upsetting, especially when you are as bossy as I am, because the combination of the bossiness and wearing shorts makes you go, 'Come on everyone, it's time we went out now, come on let's all have some fun,' and you sort of look round and they actually hate you on holiday.*
>
> Jenny Eclair

In contrast, middle-aged men on a beach aren't known for their coyness. They go in for the shorts big time. They know no one is eyeing them up any more so throw caution to the wind, letting it all hang out for everyone to see. Then they confound the problem with their footwear: they go in for the socks-and-sandals look, which looks good – on scouts.

> *I mean, that is one of the things that women care so much more about – how we look on the beach; but the men really don't mind ... There's rarely a moment when a man thinks, I don't think I should wear shorts any more. Whereas we sort of think, no more bikinis, there are men of a certain age who should think, maybe I should wear a chino slack, a cotton down-to-the-ground trouser thing, but no, they get out their old varicose veins and flash them to the world.*
>
> Jenny Eclair

I don't like men in shorts: it's not advisable. I was on a sailing holiday and a man was sitting opposite me in some tartan swimmers, which were sort of shorts, and they had a white Aertex container for the down-below bits, and may I say with the legs wide apart you could see this white sort of bandage that was keeping things together, and I just thought, I don't wish to see that. And once – this has come back to me now – the white bandage had got dislodged and there's nothing worse than seeing a little bit of something and you don't quite know what it is.

Helen Lederer

NUDISM AND TOPLESSNESS

Some people don't even bother to try to cover up: they have to go one step further and go nudist or topless. You don't know where to look for the best.

Women are unbelievable topless: the ugliest women with the most hideous bosoms and the most horrible faces, and they take their top off. Say south of France – they're lying there, like 'I am Marilyn Monroe' but they are grotesques. I think women have no idea, or maybe they say, you know, we're all equal now and I can … You know, equality of ugliness. Well, it's all very well, but I have to sit there and look at it.

People on beaches on the whole look dreadful. This includes me. Every time I go in the sea at Barbados, there are 26 paparazzi with long-focus lenses, and you know that it will appear in the papers in England – a picture of me coming out of the sea. The Mirror had a wonderful headline: 'What is large and pink and hangs from Michael Winner's shorts?' Answer: his stomach. There were about six pictures of me on the beach this year, or walking along, all with sort of fat, fat-

ter, fattest. I was fattest and I'd lost 2 stone. I was very upset, really, but these pictures continued with exactly the same captions. It doesn't matter – it's an annual bit of fun, you know.

Michael Winner

Meeting and chatting to people on a nudist beach is of course quite interesting – interesting in that you can't categorise people much at all when they don't have their clothes on to give away their class, their type, their taste and so on.

I once went to a nudist beach unknowingly on Mykonos in Greece, which is a very gay island, and I hadn't realised till I got there and went all the way to this beach, when I realised it was nothing but naked men. I was there for a while and I was quite intrigued, but actually it was quite liberating because nobody was looking at me, or I felt that nobody was comparing me with anyone else, or they were all too busy looking at each other, and I could have a jolly good look as well.

Nina Myskow

OTHER PEOPLE ON BEACHES

As usual, probably the most irritating thing about beaches is everyone else. If you could have the beach to yourself it would be a different story, but chances are if it's sunny and it's a bank holiday heading to the beach will be something a lot of other people will have also thought of, and they'll be playing radios right next to you at full blast, or kicking up the sand while playing volleyball. Or they might just be annoying full stop.

I don't go to beaches in the prime of the holiday season. A windswept cold Scottish beach, walking alone, I do, a remote beach, Australia, Mauritius – lovely, very nice. Beach, you know, Spain, France, Italy, Tenerife, millions of people, it's a glorified Ikea: I don't see the point. I may as well just be in a supermarket. No, I don't want to be with others on the beach. I don't actually like the beach.

Rhona Cameron

Truth is the fun of being on a beach is watching other people, speculating about what people do for a living, guessing how long couples have been married, or how much longer they will remain married, speculating what sort of car they drive or house they live in. Get chatting, and see whether you're right, which invariably you're not.

I'm not really a lover of beaches; I saw these people sitting there, reading books, relaxing with a nice cocktail – I can't do that, I really can't. You know, like, I'm sitting there looking at everyone to see what they're doing. What does she do for a living, then? Size of her arse she shouldn't have that on, should she? Dear oh dear, hasn't she got a mirror in her hotel room?

Linda Robson

BRITISH BEACHES

Of course the whole business of the weather becomes critical when you're on a beach. You've driven for hours to get there, you've packed a picnic, the cricket gear and a windbreak, you're committed and you've walked down 300 steps to get to it; so when it starts raining at the bottom you are forced to persevere. You get the cagoules out, you shiver: giving up or giving in to it is not an option. Not on a British beach.

A proper traditional day in a British seaside resort: you've got a light drizzle, you've got a yellow cagoule, you've got a dead jellyfish which you can nudge with a stick – yeah, that's all quite good, that's quite good as long as you know there's going to be a nice meal and some alcohol at the end of the day.

Jenny Eclair

Swimming in the sea wherever you are is fraught with worry – we've all seen *Jaws* – and even on a British beach where the risk of man-eating sharks is almost nil (although in Cornwall or the Scilly Isles I might be cautious) swimming is troublesome. British sea is for looking at or, possibly, paddling in with toddlers, not for swimming in, unless you are a cross-Channel swimmer smeared in lard.

When I look at beach water and I see icicles floating by, I don't need to even step in it, no.

Jenni Trent Hughes

I had so many childhoods where it was, 'Right, come on, we're going to the beach.' 'But it's raining, it's raining and it's grey sky and thick cloud.' 'Yes, but we're going to the beach. It's July and we're going.' And you sit there and you've got four anoraks on and the windbreakers sort of built into a box, so basically you are sitting inside a windbreaker box and drinking hot coffee, and my mother would be going, 'Isn't this marvellous? Oh, it's lovely. isn't it?' Great British summer – mad.

Jane Moore

Of course your parents were probably after a fresh-air fix, that being something that happens to you once you get older, or it does in my experience. Now I am well into middle age I am obsessed with fresh air, opening windows and telling the kids to stop watching telly because it's 'too nice a day to be indoors', or that they need some fresh air. Not that any of it registers or works at all: they don't get it; they really don't get the fresh air thing at all. So picnics in the bracing fresh air on a British beach sheltering in the windbreaks would actually in many ways be my idea of fun now, making me feel fabulously blown about in the air, but of course no one else in the family would understand and they'd moan endlessly about it. Or if they were teeny weeny kids they'd probably start to go blue with the cold, so that would spoil it for us oldies good and proper.

> *I cannot believe I am the owner of a bloody windbreak. I've got a windbreak. I used to go on demos, I used to shout angry things against Thatcher and now I go on holiday and put windbreaks up. Such is life.*
>
> *John O'Farrell*

One way or another beaches are challenging, except for that one day when the sky is cloudless and the breeze is refreshing, and everyone is getting on famously and you have a comfy place to lie and a good book to read. But for the grumpy that sort of bliss will only last for half an hour.

> *Well, of course when I was young we went to British seaside towns and they were very charming, but I don't know any that are charming now. You know, I went to a wedding in Norfolk the other day and I stayed in some strange hotel where all the rooms were decorated with Zulu shields. They had these wonderful beaches – well, you had to walk a mile to get to the beach over slush and mush. You get to this beach, and it's just a beach: there's no one serving Pina Coladas, there's no one serving tea, there's no waiters. I mean, you've got to have waiters if you have a beach; you can't have a beach without staff – it's ridiculous.*
>
> *Michael Winner*

Maybe the trick is, for the grumpily disposed, not to expect much from a beach: to simply find a nice spot out of the wind, a Cornish ice cream cornet, have a look out to sea and some fresh sea air, work up an appetite for supper, stroll along the front and saunter back to your hotel. Bournemouth, Weston-super-Mare, that sort of thing. At least you won't have forked out a small fortune, and frankly if the whole thing is more disappointing than you can bear, or the weather turns unseasonably nasty, you can always consider driving home.

9
Ambitious Holidays

Some people choose to approach holidays as if they're doing a module in the Open University. Immersing themselves in ancient history or marine biology, they go on a holiday which is crammed full of sightseeing, crammed absolutely full from morning till night with tour guides, early starts, audio visual demonstrations and bumpy treks in four-wheel-drive trucks to unspeakably out of the way places. It all sounds fun when you read about the holiday in the blurb. Well, I say fun, but that would be misleading: it sounds interesting, as if it's something you should try, now you are a grown-up and middle aged, or on an educationally sound holiday that you should take the kids on. And get there, after a year of working hard to pay for it and then the journey from hell, look at the itinerary and your heart may well sink.

You have signed up for a fortnight that crams in four dynasties and a crash course in hieroglyphics, hours and hours and hours of trudging round ruins and temples and monuments in the blistering heat with a guide who drones on and bores you rigid, be honest. There's precious little running water, the loos are

THE WORST PLACES IN THE WORLD FOR SANITATION PROVISION

The following are the worst places in terms of the percentage of population lacking access to sanitation:

- Ethiopia
- Afghanistan
- Chad
- Congo
- Eritrea
- Burkina Faso
- Niger
- Guinea
- Cambodia
- Comoros
- Lao People's Democratic Republic
- India, Angola, Namibia and Yemen

Put another way, the worst places in the world for sanitation in terms of the total number of people lacking sanitation are as follows:

- India
- China
- Indonesia
- Nigeria
- Bangladesh
- Ethiopia
- Pakistan
- Vietnam
- Brazil
- Congo

unspeakable and the food is dodgy. Well, you wanted to sample another culture – what do you expect?

> *I have friends that do all of that kind of stuff, you know, and take their orienteering maps and this and research the subject, get the old Lonely Planet guide out and we're going to go to this obscure bit and that obscure bit – no, me, where's the nicest hotel, where's the nearest bar, sorted, thank you very much, and is it hot?*
>
> Jane Moore

> *Castles, ruins, museums, art galleries – things that there are actually in your own city and your own town but you've never been to because you're not really especially interested. Because you're in another city, another town, another country, you feel you have to do all of them, and what can be more boring than walking very, very slowly round your umpteenth cathedral in Latin America looking at ghastly seventeenth-century Spanish Catholic religious art, being lectured at by a guide who can't speak English? It's not something that anybody in Peru would want to do. Why should you want to do it, because you're in Peru?*
>
> Matthew Parris

Chances are much of the stunning prehistoric or ancient history is situated in some of the poorest places on earth, so much of the holiday is spent effectively taking a look out of the window at poor people, in poor houses who don't seem to be benefiting from the coachloads of rich Westerners who have come to pay homage.

Inevitably with this sort of holiday, the loo crisis is constant, unless you are in your own hotel room, and even then the hotel might be a bit dodgy; you are going to be worrying about what the loos are going to be like from morning to night. Go to China and you might find you are expected basically to sit on the top of a hole in the ground; go to some parts of Africa and you will be sitting on a bucket, literally. You might have to go somewhere so bad, so appallingly shockingly bad that you have to hold your nose and run out. You might have to squat, balance, aim and generally see things that you will not forget in a hurry. You'll run out of Wet Wipes, you'll fret about toilet-transmitted diseases, you'll go to loos that don't flush – never flushed – and you'll subject yourself to live like 42 per cent of the world's population who are without hygienic toilets – but guess what, you paid good money for the experience. Then, predictably with a Third World sight-seeing adventure, the diarrhoea happens. It might be on day four or day six, or indeed on the flight home, but without flushing clean loos at hand 24/7, your holiday is going to become a bit of nightmare.

Tragically all the worst places for sanitation probably have the best beaches and some of the most wonderful natural sights in the world. Which isn't really fair. Trains in some of these countries are worth mentioning, of course, on the toilet front; anyone who has experienced a rock-and-roll-type loo on a train, which is basically a hole in the bottom of the train with two foot-pads, is in for something of a life-changing-nightmare-type experience. Especially when the trains jiggle about as they do. Enough said.

I can't help thinking that natural phenomena are the best sights to see rather than trudging around endless museums or catacombs. The things that might be worth all the hassle might be the stunning wonders of the world like the Niagara Falls, Ayers Rock and Lake Titicaca, wherever that is (but isn't it a wonderful name?). That sort of thing, the kind of awesome sight that takes your breath away, means you are out in the outdoors and might be able to stand and stare at for a bit.

Rather than trudging around endless museums or catacombs.

I went to Florence, went to Rome, you know, the Coliseum, you know, the Sistine Chapel and I just didn't appreciate it. I feel that these things should be bringing me happiness and, and I think I am deeply flawed that they don't but they just don't.

Rhona Cameron

I'm good for about 20, 25 minutes, really, at a ruin and then I want to get out fast.

Kathryn Flett

Alas, the coach will not be due to pick you up for another hour and five minutes.

CRUISES

You could always go on a floating coach tour and sightsee that way instead: go on a cruise. People do still go on them, apparently. They were all the rage in the 1970s, it seemed, the very last word in exotic luxurious holidays and a splendid way to spend the inheritance before your children get hold of it, I suppose. Marvellous for the idle sightseer, which includes me; in fact I have no idea why I have never thought of going on one. Settling down into your own comfort zone, unpacking for a fortnight instead of packing up every couple of days, sitting on deck, bags of sea air and then docking to see some lovely places now and again – sounds good. Trouble is – well, one of the troubles – that unlike on dry land, you chum up with some people who are over-friendly or you find yourself in entertainment hell (both of which are distinct possibilities, I would imagine), and there's no getting away, as in no getting away at all, because guess what: you are all in the same boat, literally.

A cruise is my idea of triple, quadruple nightmare. Can you imagine being on a boat with thousands of people? A very wonderful concierge at the Splendido Portofino went on a cruise. He said it was a nightmare. To get off you have a number; they gave you a number because you couldn't all get off at once – 2,000 people, and you sat waiting for your number to be called before you could go down the gangplank. Getting off could take two or three hours.

Michael Winner

The docking bit, of course, would worry me, since whenever I have seen cruise ships docked they seem to be docked in the nastiest Chernobyl-like ports, not quaint harbours, and are by definition a coach ride away from the interesting bits. And you can bet your bottom dollar that the tour organisers have some hideously sordid arrangement with the local souvenir sellers, which means you are coached to a big shop selling parchment drawings or Chinese glass or something else you will get home and wish you hadn't bought, but because the coach was there for a clever 40 minutes you went and bought one.

And imagine the sun-lounger war on a cruise: three coaches of people heading back to the ship after the sightseeing for the morning, to the tiny pool, and all six hundred of you wanting to loll in peace and quiet. There would be injuries, I imagine.

I don't want to be trapped with people; I don't want to be trapped with anybody, I am extremely anti-social. You know, I keep getting offered these free cruises. 'Make two speeches, Mr Winner, and we'll take you to New York, we'll take you; make a speech every week and sign a few autographs and you can have it free.' Free? I'd pay not to go on it.

Michael Winner

Peace and quiet, from what I hear, on cruises would be tricky. All that laid-on entertainment, theme nights – probably find your-self on a boat with Cilla Black doing cabaret or Bobby Davro doing the comedy routine.

The odd nice meal on a holiday, yes OK. But on a cruise you have to shift so many meals you're rarely not eating. Let up for one meal and there's a backlog of food to shift – duck à l'orange, baked Alaska, prawn cocktail, and that's before elevenses. They *make* you eat, presumably; it's an eating holiday. Miracle they stay afloat.

> *They start with a buffet breakfast and, you know, there's everything you can think of. You then have a lunch. Meanwhile while the lunch buffet is going on there's like a little parlour thing that opens, selling pizza and hot dogs and burgers, so straight away as soon as the Americans have had the buffet lunch they go straight out and get the pizzas. I mean, they are like savages, honestly, queuing up for this – well, not even queuing up, knocking each other out of the way to get to the burgers, the hot dogs and the piz-zas. And then they have an afternoon tea thing with sand-wiches and cakes and whatever, and then you have your evening meal and then about 11 o'clock at night you have this chocolate feast thing. It's like this sort of great big – oh, it's like a Disneyland sort of feature where they've got all melted chocolate or chocolate cakes. I mean, honestly, it is unbelievable, the food, and of course they have to eat every-thing.*
>
> Linda Robson

Of course you could go the yacht route. Pretend you're in *Heat* magazine; swank about.

> *I never wish to go on a yacht; I never wish to sleep on a yacht. I'm not even happy going on yacht just for dinner, quite hon-*

estly, cos I can't get up and walk away; I can't walk away and I'll sink the end of the boat. I can't suddenly say 'I'm feeling a bit strange now, I think I'll go to my room,' cos you're in the sea. The sea is not a place for me.

Michael Winner

Then there would be the seasickness to worry about on a holiday cruise or yacht. As holiday anxieties go, this would be a fairly serious one, it seems to me. Like doing the cross-Channel ferry all holiday, non-stop.

THE BRITISH ABROAD

Maybe as a nation, sightseeing and travelling abroad do not come naturally to us. The truth is that on the whole most of us wouldn't bother to go abroad if it were not for one thing: the weather. Cornwall, Scotland and Northumberland are spectacularly beautiful, with beaches and coastlines to die for, and if only the weather were more predictable (good) then frankly most of us would not be that fussed about going abroad much at all. Britain being an island, of course going abroad (or to the Continent, as we used to call it) is still relatively inconvenient. It's

---

THE WORLD'S TOP TOURISM DESTINATIONS

- France 9.8 per cent market share
- Spain 6.9 per cent
- USA 6.0 per cent
- China 5.5 per cent
- Italy 4.9 per cent
- UK 3.6 per cent

not like in Europe, where you can drive over the border from France to Italy and not notice; with us you have to inconvenience yourself somewhat. When I say somewhat, I mean sometimes at considerable expense and inconvenience, and we have to subject ourselves to massive cultural differences, like going to a country where they don't have kettles or where they don't do proper pillows or gravy.

But illogical and inconvenient as it is, in fact we now like going abroad so much so that 5.5 million British nationals live overseas permanently – the equivalent of 9.2 per cent of the UK's population. In addition an estimated 500,000 British people live abroad for part of the year, mainly through second home ownership. Nearly one in ten British nationals lives for part or all of the year abroad. Top destinations for emigration are Australia, Spain, US, Canada, Ireland, New Zealand, South Africa, France, Germany and Cyprus in that order.

When we British go abroad we do all those things which very foreign people like Americans do when they come to Europe: we cling together, we either literally or metaphorically put up flags, we take our food and drink with us, and then we throw it all up again all over the pavement.

Not that going or living abroad means necessarily that we go native. When we're abroad we seem, more than most nations, to remain so conspicuously British, so fiercely nationalistic, so determined to defend our own culture or indeed impose it on everyone else, so ludicrous in our khaki shorts, so bossy in our missionary role and, if today is anything to go by, frankly so drunk that it's no wonder that natives took cover when they saw us coming rather than try to take us on all those years ago when we were conquering the British Empire.

When the British Empire was founded, I've sort of come to understand how they did it. They must have just got off the

boat like any other British holiday maker in their Union Jack shorts, with their lagers in their hands going, 'Hey, we're going to have a great time,' and the natives would have run in terror, and saying, you know, 'We're going to keep well out of the way.' I'm not surprised the Zulus ended up being defeated by the British army, because if you see a load of lads clutching lager bottles at ten in the morning you want to keep well out of their way, and that's basically what the British army was *like throughout the colonial period, and that's why we ended up dominating the globe, because no one wanted to take them on, I tell you.*

John O'Farrell

Our determination to stick together and to remain entirely British at all times is reflected in the fact that we are so feeble in our attempts to speak the native language. It wasn't until very recently that I realised that in fact Spanish is the most common language in the world, not English at all. I had always assumed that our idleness to learn any other language had at least some logic in it: that we spoke the most spoken language in the world and so it made sense for everyone else to keep up. Which puts our shameful inability to speak Spanish when we go to Spain into perspective.

Nearly a quarter of British travellers apparently do not even know what language is spoken at their holiday destination and a third do not learn the basics of how to say hello, please, thank you and goodbye when holidaying in a non-English-speaking country.

Mind you, even if you do struggle to speak a few basic words of their language, the locals often humiliate us, taking their revenge for having to put up with our drinking and unspeakably rude acts on the beach. They watch you struggling with your pidgin French or Spanish or Greek as you order a dry white wine, and then promptly reply to you in their impeccable English.

It's clear that the British are not much interested in the culture of the country they're visiting. In fact you'd be forgiven for thinking that the British don't actually like being abroad at all, and would do anything to trick themselves into thinking they are in fact in Blackpool in a heatwave, not actually in Tenerife at all (although having been to Tenerife recently, I can to some extent understand this head-in-sand mentality – if you could find some sand, that is) and the British congregate en masse to such an extent, let's face it, you'd be lucky to find someone Spanish in some parts of Spain.

Are Brits too British abroad?

According to a recent survey:

- 50 per cent of Britons snub local cuisine in favour of good old fish and chips and English breakfasts.
- 14 per cent of men take their home football team's shirt with them.
- 34 per cent of British people take their umbrellas.
- 1 per cent even take English tea bags to ensure they don't miss out on a good brew.

We could have told them that for free.

Of course the sophisticated grumpy person is tourist impeccable, but even middle-aged grumpy people who are a model of behaviour, politeness and cultural diplomacy – even we can't bear to be severed from the beloved English papers for long. For some reason we travel thousands of miles to get away from the daily routine and immerse ourselves in a different culture yet spend half the time trying to find yesterday's newspaper, paying £5 for it in order to read about last night's telly.

I do like English newspapers, particularly the Sunday papers – the scandal, I like to read a bit of scandal wherever I am; and of course you love to read the weather's terrible, you love to turn to the weather, weather in London rain, weather in London storms – marvellous. You're in the sun, you know, phone anybody and if they say what's the weather, if they say in London the weather's good, you think, I'm depressed for the rest of the day.

Michael Winner

This sort of one-upmanship is admittedly not confined to reading the papers. Hence people send you showy-offy postcards from the Caribbean in January, not because they are keen to give you interesting news, or to tell you they are missing you (although they might pretend that is their aim): no, they send you such a postcard to show off, to tell you, 'I'm somewhere sunny and gorgeous and you're not; I'm on a yacht and you're not.'

Of course another reason that so many British holiday abroad, apart from our unspeakable weather, is that things are frankly cheaper. On the whole the restaurants are cheaper, and alas the booze is a great deal cheaper. Enough said ...

I think the thing is that you know where to avoid. If you don't want to mix with, let's just say, common people on holiday then you don't go to those places. Mind you, you know, even sort of quite sophisticated places like Prague have been taken over basically by the stag and hen thing, so you get on a flight to Prague and you realise that you are the oldest person on that flight by some years. Of course you come back sort of the end of the weekend and you're on the same flight as all those young revellers and they're in a very sorry condition, they really are. I quite like that.

Jenny Eclair

I am so ashamed of other British people, all over the world, wherever I go. Mean people, rude people, people who don't want to see the glories of the country where they are, people complaining about the food and asking for fish and chips, people drinking too much and getting sick all over the place, and I think to myself, How were those people ever allowed a

> *passport? Hell, you have to have a nationality test these days if you want to take out British nationality to prove that you're a fit person. I think you should have to have a test to leave this country with British nationality. I think there should be examinations before you're allowed to have a passport to show that you are a fit and proper person to represent your nation abroad.*
>
> Matthew Parris

Since we take our nationality away on holiday with us for all to see, it will come as no surprise that we take our football with us wherever we go too. And football, of course, brings out the most British Britishness in us – a bad combination all round.

Interestingly Brits hate other Brits when they are on holiday more than anything else. A survey has shown that one of the biggest irritants for the British abroad is, umm, the British abroad. 39 per cent of travellers say that Brits annoy them when they are abroad. The top three most annoying elements of a bad holiday are delayed or cancelled flights, the British abroad and foreign touts.

Holiday Brits have admitted they are a disgrace abroad. In a survey, 98 per cent of people said Britons let the country down in the eyes of foreigners.

Drunken behaviour on a plane or in a resort tops the list of shameful behaviour, according to nine in ten people. More than six in ten said not trying to speak the language in holiday spots like Spain was our second worst vice. Sexual antics in public upset 55 per cent of people. Badly behaved children, a failure to explore beyond the tourist resort and insisting on British food were also pet hates.

Londoners felt most strongly that Brits are a menace abroad, while Geordies were the most relaxed about the problem. Younger people tended to be the most easy-going about sexual behaviour. Well, there's a surprise then.

Ten ways Brits disgrace themselves on holiday:

1. Drunken behaviour on plane or in resort
2. Not trying to speak the local language
3. Public sexual antics
4. Badly behaved children
5. Failing to explore beyond the resort
6. Getting sunburnt
7. Playing loud music at beach/pool
8. Ordering English food in restaurants
9. Inappropriate clothes
10. Fighting over sunbeds

HOW TO SPOT THE BRITISH ABROAD

There are other tell-tale signs of the British abroad. We eat the moment we are on the move: as soon as the train or boat moves off we British open our sandwiches. We lug back litre bottles of mineral water from the grocery store to our rooms even though the store is a bus ride away – anything rather than open the mini bar.

> You could spot a Brit on holiday straight away, cos usually we are kind of blue, cos we never see the sun. This obsession where everybody wears football kits – even the baby is in a football kit; the mum, the dad, the kids, they are all in a football kit, and the dad has got a beer gut and you just think, You have not played football since Bobby Moore was captain. We are

*obsessed with wearing sports gear on holiday and yet look like
the least-sports-playing nation.*

Jane Moore

*I don't think it is good when you see the families in the
England tops, and that includes the women, and it's often, you
know, that sort of fat, bald, salmon-pink-type Englishman,
you know – all look like Phil Mitchell. Then there's often three
generations of England tops, isn't there? There's a granddad,
who is like a thinner version, there's a big fat beefy salmon-
pink Phil Mitchell father and then there's miniature little, on
his way to being beefy salmon-pink miniature Phil Mitchell
England top little boy. That's depressing when you see it across
the three generations.*

Rhona Cameron

Not that we're the only nation to blob out when we get a little bit
older. One minute we're leggy lovelies in teeny weeny polka dot
bikinis and the next we're in that ad rolling out pizza for our
family of twelve on our ample bosoms only partially covered by a
pinny.

*You can't win anywhere if you are a British woman over 25, I
don't think. But we beat the Greeks: quite pretty when they are
young, but boy do they go off – they sort of disappear, don't
they, at about 23 and then next time you see them they've got
no teeth and a donkey on a string. Who else are we competing
against? No, I mean, well, enough has been said about the
Germans, I am not going to add to that because it's a cliché,
but it's only a cliché because it's true.*

Jenny Eclair

FOREIGN FOOD

We like foreign food: we probably have more Italian food here than they do in Italy and more taramasalata than they have in Greece, and certainly we have more French fries than they have in the whole of France and I've never even been able to find any French mustard in France whatsoever. But foreign food abroad is something different, and it can be challenging for the British, which is presumably why so many take their own food with them or insist on ordering British food when they're there. For one thing, being a vegetarian abroad, especially in France, is a bit tricky. They don't really do vegetarian food – don't do many vegetables at all, really. Ask for the vegetarian option and they'll offer you fish; tell them you don't eat fish and they look puzzled and say, 'Well, what do you eat? The grass?' They have such a lovely way with them sometimes, the French. French women eat chocolate, apparently, endlessly showing off about it and the fact that they still remain a slim size 12. But it beats me how they stay so healthy on it all. Even finding wholemeal bread is a challenge in France. I saw a loaf in a chemist's window last time I went: it looked as if it was only available on prescription.

> I think the food abroad is generally pretty good unless you go somewhere like Austria. When I went there when I was a vegetarian, it was like, 'You can have sausage soup or you can have sausages or you can have chopped up sausages or more sausages.'
>
> John O'Farrell

DRIVING ABROAD

One thing that is properly challenging about leaving this country is driving on the right-hand side of the road. You'd think we'd

- Half UK motorists drive abroad without checking their insurance.
- 46 per cent of motorists break European driving regulations.
- Over half a million Brits don't know the speed limits of foreign roads.
- 46 per cent of motorists are driving illegally when in Europe, by not carrying a warning triangle in their car.

take that relatively seriously but alas, apparently Brits abroad are often uninsured, unprepared and unsure what to do on foreign roads.

THE HOLIDAY SNAPS

Whatever kind of holiday you do, before you can contemplate going home you have to record your marvellous adventure for eternity. You've seen the leaning tower of Pisa or Capitol Hill, but unless you photograph it – taking dozens of meaningless shots that no one at all will find interesting in the slightest – or worse, you record it all on video, it doesn't count.

All that trouble you went to and the truth is you'll get home and fling them all in the photo cupboard, the one stuffed full of the last 15 years' worth of holiday snaps which you keep meaning to sort out and never get round to. You can set aside a fortnight and still at the end of it be finding negatives from Burnham-on-Sea in 1978. And you could have saved yourself a lot of fuss and bother and lugging around the home video camera, as most of the hours of footage is out of focus or shot by mistake or hideously unwatchable, making you feel nauseous – you're not going to be watching this again in a hurry. Perhaps, as they say, you had to be there.

Have you ever been on holiday with a keen photographer?
They might as well not have been on the holiday at all, because
they never enjoy anything as they're just snap, snap, snapping
all the time. You have to get out of the way, you have to pose
here, you have to pose there; no sooner do they see what looks
like an interesting scene than out comes the camera and the
whole business of professional photography begins. It spoils
the real experience of seeing things with your own eyes for the
first time.

Matthew Parris

I give pretty short shrift these days to the production of holiday
photos. I'll say something like, 'I'll give you 30 seconds and no
more, and no anecdotes – get straight to the point.' Some of the
dullest, most excruciating memories I have of being a teenager
are when slides were all the rage and people would go the whole
hog, putting the lights out and treating you to a full 90-minute
show on their mini break in Amsterdam. Not only did they feel
they had to explain every slide, but the dreaded words 'You can't
see it on this photo but just around the corner …' would mean yet
more time on the slide and more information that was too much
information. But people do still sometimes try to show you photos or try to tell you about their holiday. Other people's holidays
are like other people's dreams. Not interesting at all. So get over
it.

Do you remember in the olden days when you used to get them
back from the chemist … For some reason you really wanted
to look at them then, could hardly wait to get back in the car
– oh, the excitement! You'd rip them open and you've just got
shot after shot of some sort of red raw drunken slag stuck to a
plastic chair, and then you realise, ooh, that's me, and I
always look a bit like sort of Jimmy Saville that's been boiled
like a lobster and that's very, very depressing. You don't look

at other people's holiday photos – not unless you're in them.
There's no point, is there?

Jenny Eclair

Well, if you're not even interested in your own holiday photo-
graphs, why would you be interested in someone else's, even if
you love them, even if they're your dear, dear friend? You've
all been to kind of the same places. Unless you have had a truly
extraordinary holiday, and been abducted or been involved in
some sort of terrorist activity or something inadvertently,
then really nobody's really remotely interested in ever seeing
your snaps.

Kathryn Flett

My dad writes in biro, you know, 'Abergavenny, October
1978', and they are all there, you know, and he can put down
like, 'local man/local trader (smiling)'. But I always start off
with good intentions and do four of those and then the rest are
just a random collection of kind of toothless people with tan-
gerines on barrows.

Stuart Maconie

10

Skiing and other death-defying pursuits

Sometimes otherwise rational, logical human beings sign up for the sort of holiday that an alien would (understandably) consider baffling to bonkers. Here's the general idea: throw yourself down the side of a mountain on a pair of slippy planks, risk death or maiming, and then spend an hour and a half getting back to the top of the mountain again and jostling with irritating French teenagers in the freezing cold to do it all over again – all day long. Presumably if you embark on such a holiday it is because you wanted something different holiday-wise: you were fed up with the sun, sand and sea scenario. You wanted activity. Why you couldn't just make do with the kind of activity that involves walking to a nice restaurant for lunch is beyond me, or even just walking in the Alpine air and marvelling at the snow-capped mountains from a rooftop café with a nice cappuccino and a pastry.

The irresistible Alpine air, the swish of the snow, slaloming past snow-capped mountains, feeling on top of the world, literally – skiing has its appeal, I suppose, and maybe it's not so hard. I

We're seriously considering a skiing holiday – do you have anyone here who could talk us out of it?

mean, little children can ski, so maybe anyone can do it: a little patience, a little old-fashioned stamina and you're off. Alas, it is so not easy, especially for someone over 15. Getting going isn't the problem; it's getting stopped – that's the tricky bit. Get it wrong and the only way to stop is to hurl yourself into the nearest snowdrift or bush, or a queue of other skiers. It looks so effortlessly easy when the instructors do it, but it is like learning to drive in the fast lane of the M6 without the benefit of a brake pedal. The idea of being back at work suddenly feels quite restful.

You knew it would be energetic, but the whole business of skiing is hassle from morning to night, with a lot of pushing and shoving. And it's not as if you can just think, Oh goody, I might do a spot of skiing today: the whole palaver of getting kitted out and putting on huge clodhopping boots that give you blisters when you trudge around in them takes you so long you only have an hour or two left to ski at all – which might, come to think of it, be a blessing.

> *I found the stuff, the stuff involved, the getting up in the morning, the faffing, the putting on all the things, the layers, the fashion crisis of it, wrapping yourself in condoms, really, effectively, and the layering things, because it might start off blizzard conditions and it might end up like the Caribbean and you have to be prepared – even though I'm a woman who packs to be prepared, this really can stretch you. And then it's exhausting; it's absolutely exhausting. And for those of us who go on holiday not to be exhausted, it's a shock to the system.*
>
> *Kathryn Flett*

> *It's fucking freezing and you look like a lagged boiler. I mean, what's the point of that? You know, so you come home with a suntanned face and the rest of you pale, what's the point of that, and a broken leg.*
>
> *Nina Myskow*

And you thought a beach holiday was tricky clothes-wise: that a costume and a nice big sarong was challenging. Wait until you get the padded ski wear on.

The Ski Lift Crisis

As holidays go, the fashion crisis of a skiing holiday is a distinct disadvantage, it has to be said, as is the exhausting-to-the-point-of-having-trouble-staying-awake-beyond-8-p.m. aspect, but for me the thing about skiing that is the hardest to marry with the word 'holiday' is the anxiety. The first anxiety attack happens when you see the monstrous contraptions to get you and your silly skis to the top. Have you seen the ski lifts, or the teeny weeny cable cars that dangle over drops the size of the Eiffel Tower?

And have you been in one with a teenager who is larking about and making it rock because he thinks it's funny? Or have you been on one of those ski lifts that you sit in with just a lap belt to keep you in, which makes the big wheel at the scariest of travelling fairs look like a little Postman Pat ride? And have you been on lifts when they bump and jolt over the cable pylons, or when they have a temporary fault and they leave you dangling for 40 minutes, desperate for a pooh because your adrenalin has kicked in with an anxiety attack?

And lose your buttock grip on a button lift on the bit of cast iron and you'll be stranded halfway up or find yourself dangling from a Meccano set at a height of 3,000 feet. Either way, suddenly you wish you were on a sun-lounger in Sorrento.

> *I love skiing and one of my favourite things of all is watching people trying to get on a button lift, which is like this smallest, smallest button like this and you have to … And it keeps coming around like this, like a sort of moving tie rack, and you have to position yourself and get this button between your legs and clamp your legs together like that, and then off you go. You just see all these people that … myself included, I might add. The first three times I completely went flying in front of everyone.*
>
> *Jane Moore*

And that's before you even try to get off the thing. Getting off one of the contraptions in your skis, with your poles, is of course both terrifying and horribly inevitable once you have committed yourself and got on it. Nice. All nice.

Flying by the Seat of Your Pants

Getting up and down the mountains is spookily like a bad day at Tesco, but with the added excitement of taking your life into your hands. And the cherry on the cake is that once you've got up there and you have managed to get down alive, assuming you do, then you're expected to do the same thing over and over and over again.

Get yourself on the ski run itself, and suddenly all the other skiers are going at 40 miles an hour, and smart-arse boy racers are skimming you and making you wobble and fall over. You'll be lucky to get back home without needing a fracture clinic.

> *I did break my arm, actually, skiing, although strictly speaking I didn't break my arm: a very fat man sat on it. I was coming down a hill, quite efficiently actually, and he was crossing the hill, and he was proper huge, I mean proper, proper huge, sort of three seats on an aeroplane huge, and he bumped into me. We sort of wobbled a bit, and then I went, 'No, no, no you're all right,' and then he kind of came towards me and I sort of went back, and I went that way to get away from him, and he sat on my arm and it broke in 16 places. I don't know why I'm laughing. It was very sore. I suppose it was better than sitting on my chest and squeezing me to death. So that was strictly speaking not a skiing injury, but it did happen on a slope.*
>
> *Arabella Weir*

Learning to ski when you are an adult isn't just difficult: it's impossible. Unless you have been skiing since you were four you are basically stuck with just going where the skis want to take you. It might be over the edge of the precipice, it might be down the blackest, hardest run – who knows? Just standing up feels dangerous, the nursery slopes feel dangerous and the ski runs themselves look so treacherous they should be illegal. No wonder some people throw the towel in, take the skis back to the ski hire and basically chill out in front of a nice fire. Everyone else can risk death or near-death injury all day in the perishing cold…

A skiing holiday doesn't bother me as long as there is a fire-place, a very big sofa and some sort of hot tub outside; I want to see the snow, I like the snow, but as for putting two pieces of wood on the bottom of my feet and flinging myself down the side of a mountain, I don't think so, no.

Jenni Trent Hughes

I go to ski resorts, like Gstaad, but I don't ski, I go up in the ski lift, cos there are very nice views from the ski lift. I get off at the top of the ski lift, I look around and I get back and go down again, so I'm the only person in the ski lift without skis – all these skiers going up and down, they've all got skis, they've got boots, you know, and I've got nothing, I'm just having a trip. Sometimes we'll have lunch at the top of the ski lift and go back.

Michael Winner

Generally I have never seen the attraction of skiing. I suppose because if I want to see people falling over, get harangued by drunken women in the freezing cold, taking my life in my hands, I can do that in Doncaster. I don't need to go to Grenoble.

Stuart Maconie

What Jolly Hooray Henry Fun

On top of all this, on top of all this frankly shockingly off-putting information, the whole holiday is vastly expensive and full of people who evidently have more money than sense. Worse still, it attracts young people with money, posh public-school-boy types or girls called Giles and Abigail who have been to absurdly expensive public schools, and who winter as chalet maids and have never even seen a raw potato in their life, never mind know how to run house for 16 hungry holiday makers. Skiing attracts a lot of posh people who have been skiing since kindergarten, who hooray and guffaw and show off in their designer ski wear and with their fancy swanky moves and are very annoying indeed.

> *All those kind of hoorays, you know, go and live in Gstaad or wherever for the season and do a lot of, 'Yeah, I'm cooking my way through my skiing holiday' – when you see a bunch of them, come on, you wanker, going down the hills, you just think, Ah, let's just hope they go over the edge.*
>
> Arabella Weir

Aprés Ski

I'm told the après ski is a riot – really worth writing home about. Not that I have ever seen any of it. At all. The two times I went skiing I was so completely spent and exhausted by the time I had finished a couple of runs down the slopes that I was in need of Ralgex, a hot bath and my bed by 7.45 p.m. But honestly I can't see that any holiday nightlife that revolves around Abigail, Giles, their toffee-nosed mates and a cheese fondue can be anything other than unappealing to the point of shocking. Get really unlucky and you might be somewhere where they've booked a load of blokes in lederhosen to slap their thighs and generally dominate the restaurant. Getting the picture?

> *You see in the brochure the sitting round the log fire, drinking Glühwein, but it's like you're just basically putting various creams on bruises and re-dressing the wounds every evening and going out with the kids, who, you know, want to have snowball fights and do tobogganing, and you're limping behind them cos you've put your knee out of joint. Basically*

it's a way of ageing ten years in a week and paying a lot of money for it.

John O'Farrell

On the Pissed

And if you are still undecided about whether to go skiing – still feeling you might chance it, and that it can't be that bad or that dangerous – I will remind you that lot of people are in fact under the influence of alcohol when they are skiing. Put that in your pipe and smoke it.

ACTIVITY HOLIDAYS

The growing popularity of activity holidays is irrefutable: evidently many of us are keen to throw ourselves off mountains, sky dive, bungee jump or learn to rock climb. All such activities sound marvellously exciting. Trouble is you might get there and after day two realise that rock climbing is not for you, to the point of giving you a funny turn; or, as in my own case, you might go on a fortnight's canoeing holiday and discover after lunch on day one when you have turned the boat over and capsized that you should never be allowed in a canoe again, because you are such a danger to other canoeists, and because of your terror and incompetence (bad combination), which mean you are likely to end up with your boat at right angles to the riverbank and cause motorway-like pile-ups of canoes all day. Surely some of these activity holidays should come with a basic skill requirement before you are allowed to book them – something to protect us from our own over-enthusiasm?

I was with my then boyfriend, and we boldly booked a day's white water rafting down the Zambezi, which I have to say is

about seven hours too much. And I had to get out at lunchtime and go home, back to the hotel and order a lot of cocktails. And drink them in quick succession. It was absolutely the most terrifying thing ever, because of the thing they do on these white water rafting is, so you don't feel you've been ripped off after paying all this money, they ensure that you get wet, and they do this by flipping the boat so that you have a sort of drowning experience.   *Kathryn Flett*

You could do a cycling holiday, sauntering along lovely quiet Danish or French roads from one hotel to the next, and have a marvellous time in the fresh air. But I know what would happen in my case, I would intend to do some training, intend to get around to doing some weekend cycling, but never get around to it, and then on day two I would be so saddle sore that I would become a major liability and have to put the bike in the support truck and spend the week waiting for everyone else to catch up.

Personally I think Michael Winner has it sussed; I think he should give masterclasses in taking holidays. I just hope I never have to compete for a sun-lounger with him.

I do not have activity holidays. For me activity is raising the beach flag in order to get the Pina Colada. That is activity, waving the flag. Believe me, I'm exhausted.

                                              Michael Winner

11

Holidays, who needs them?

Little bits of unpredicted jollity, the odd lovely lunch with people you love, a walk on the beach, a little corner in the sun, a favourite bench and a gorgeous view to make you feel good – such things don't seem a lot to ask for on a holiday. But as we've seen in this book, again and again holidays let us down, and are so disappointing.

> I know what the word 'holiday' is supposed to conjure up. It is supposed to conjure up an oasis of calm and serenity in the middle of a stressful life, a period where you step outside the cares of everyday life and recharge one's batteries. But in actual fact what it means to me automatically is a kind of steel band being slowly tightened around the head, or being shouted at in a language I only barely comprehend, or watching a plane I was supposed to be on slowly making its way into the sky, or endlessly looking for a bag that never turns up at a baggage carousel.
>
> Stuart Maconie

Often the failure of a holiday to deliver a grump-free time is due as much to expectations as to whether or not anything actually goes wrong on it.

> *I think the terrible thing about holidays is the fact that everybody's expected to enjoy it; I think that's why you have them. You go somewhere, it's lovely, it's sunny, you meet wonderful people and it's supposed to be fun. That's not been my experience, I have to say.*
>
> Don Warrington

> *I think you can sort of tell when it's all going to go wrong, quite early, and it may be as early as en route to the airport. And it's to do with the fact that there's so much expectation involved. You put so much effort into it, you've spent so much money, you've booked out the time, you've worked your butt off to create the space in which you can relax, so you're exhausted; maybe you've got some small children in tow, or just children, maybe you've got some ageing relatives. It's like Christmas, but worse, because at least at Christmas you're just stuck at home in your house, cooking like a nutcase. Here you're stuck in someone else's house in a foreign country, unable to get the ingredients to cook yourself out of your misery, surrounded by people that frankly, you know, you need the holiday from.*
>
> Kathryn Flett

HOLIDAYS AS CURE-ALL

Just to ramp up the odds even more, the truth is that we look forward to a holiday because we hope it is going to sort things out; we assume that the things that worry us at home are going to disappear, or that the worries we have will vanish, as if by magic, once we get on holiday. True, holidays will give you a bit of rest, if you're lucky, but post-holiday blues, like post-Christmas blues, are pretty much a given, because more or less no problem goes away because you have been on holiday.

> *Holidays can never possibly live up to what your expectations are because you want everything from a holiday and it can't be, and you always take your problems with you, and even if you don't take problems with you, your neurosis expands to fill the space available, so instead of worrying about the mortgage, you worry about, Oh, God, have I got a blister on my left foot, and you can obsess about that all day.*
>
> Nina Myskow

> *It seems to me that holidays are all about going somewhere that's different to where you live, and the problem with that is you tend to take the feelings you have where you live on the holiday, and so if you're unhappy at home you're unhappy on holiday.*
>
> Don Warrington

> *The word 'holiday' gives me an instant migraine actually. What it does is it makes me … It's a microcosm for life, isn't it, the holiday, because what it does in two weeks is remind you that life is awful and there's a huge gulf between sort of what you expect out of life and reality.*
>
> Jenny Eclair

RELAXING

Grumpy people, it seems, are quite bad at relaxing. The grumpy radar is still on wherever you are, and there are little things, and then again some big things, which are inevitably going to set you off. So that elusive relaxation is going to be hard to achieve. When you're on holiday and supposed to be profoundly relaxed, this is problematic.

> *I tend to be quite sort of tense and bad tempered. It takes a long time for the holiday spirit to infect me – a very long time, in fact. I sort of – by the time I get there I've turned into a bit of a bitch.*
>
> Jenny Eclair

Of course some people don't even try to relax on holiday. They give up, and take the office away with them to avoid the backlog when they get home.

Research revealed that vacationers 'get away' but stay connected to home and work. Laptop computers have become the new 'must have' on-the-road travel accessory, apparently.

In fact, laptops now rival mobile phones as the technological travel accessory for keeping in touch with home and work.

Yes, OK the British work too hard, and yes, they do sometimes work on hoilday, but the truth is the British spend most of their holidays gettign drunk, being drunk or recovering from being drunk.

British holidaymakers would fritter away 365,366 weeks languishing in hotel rooms with hangovers on holiday, says a survey.

They also waste 289,866 weeks being ill, 525,803 weeks planning holidays on holiday and 80,892 weeks complaining while on holiday.

SOCIALISING

Chumming up and making friends with people you meet on holiday is all very well, but it gets complicated. You meet people and then find you're avoiding them for the rest of the fortnight. You go out for dinner with them and who pays? You invite them on to your balcony and before you know it it's your turn to ask back. You might as well just be back at home, frankly, for all the complications. All this and you can't even say you're busy at work – you don't even have an exit strategy.

> *I suppose I don't go on those sort of holidays. My mum and dad do and they are always coming back and telling me, 'Oh, you know, we got saddled with this terrible couple from Bermondsey who wanted to, you know, show us their tattoos and things like that.' But fortunately, perhaps because of that, you know, I tend to be very anti-social now and sort of, you know, go and stay in a cave for two days on my own or with a close personal friend.*
>
> Stuart Maconie

Of course the friendships you make on holiday are unique. You don't know where they live, you can't really judge what sort of person they are, you can't see the car they drive or the job they do – all you have to judge from is how much ankle jewellery they're wearing, whether they sound as if they come from Dudley in the west Midlands, what books they're reading and what they *tell* you they do for a living.

Far more fun to speculate. Spend your days lolling on a sunbed wondering what the people next to you do for a living, how long they have been married and whether he or she might be having an affair. Are they in manufacturing, or a civil servant, or do they play in a band in their spare time? Either that or don't make friends at all: keep your head down.

I don't have the problem of keeping in touch with people because I, we, just don't make friends on holiday, we are so grumpy and self-contained. I mean, I'll be friendly if people talk to me, but I'm very … I don't want someone, you know, turning up on my doorstep when I get back to Britain going, 'Hi, remember us and our 25 children, we've come to stay' – no thanks.

Jane Moore

While I do think you can never know too many wonderful people, when I go on holiday I do not go on holiday to meet people. I will say hello, I will have a polite brief conversation, but I do not want to come back with a whole host of new friends; that's just not why I go on holiday, because the problem is once you start talking to them then they want to talk to you all the time, and then they want you to go on excursions with them and they want you to go places with them, and all of that is exactly what I've gone on holiday to get away from, so I pretend to be very, very boring when I go on holiday.

Jenni Trent Hughes

Next time I meet someone really dull on holiday I'll assume that he or she is like Jenni: pretending to be dull so as not to encourage me to make friends or be too chatty. I think this will make me feel more cheerful about life in general.

And of course unless you're one of those types who organise reunions, if you have met people you may prefer not to swap (correct) names and addresses at the end.

Sadly I am usually excruciatingly honest, so a couple of days before, like two days before, the very end of the holiday you can't see me or find me, because I know that's when all the phone number exchanging starts going on.

Jenni Trent Hughes

The other option is to take your existing friends with you. Which is frankly dangerous.

I like to go on holiday with friends, but every now and then you do it with some friends and it's a way of killing off the friendship for ever: if you're ever unsure about whether you're good mates or not a week together on holiday, you know, is a fantastic way of heightening the differences that you have.

John O'Farrell

However much you know your friends, love your friends, the

truth is that you are not accustomed to spending 24 hours a day with them, sharing a room and a bathroom with them, sharing a kitchen; and even if you did ever share a kitchen with them when you were young, when you made friends with them, nowadays you are unused to sharing anything with anyone. You're not used to having to put your nightie on in the bathroom or worry about letting off in front of anyone. Worse than that, you are going to want to do something – anything – at a different pace to your friend. Suddenly even the most solid, the longest of friendships are challenging.

> I used to try and go away with various girlfriends and this is a complete disaster because they always want to have cups of coffee when you don't want to have cups of coffee. They always want to buy something when you don't; they don't want to go to the museum. Then they always fall in love with the greasy waiter.
>
> Nina Myskow

Worse, they spend money in a different way to you, put less money in the kitty than you do, don't pay their way or get really stingy about everything. This is another area for potential punch-ups. Ordinarily you could laugh it off, but spend a fortnight with someone who refuses ever to buy a drink or endlessly wastes money, and the tension will mount to boiling point.

BUMPING INTO SOMEONE YOU KNOW

Bumping into someone you know when you are away on holiday is much more common than you'd think. Unless by an extraordinary stroke of luck you bump into your best friend – but then if they are your best friend you would know they were going there, of course – chances are that if you bump into someone you know it will be seriously bad news. This, of course, is much worse than making new friends on holiday, because if you're on holiday and you meet your boss or your boss's boss or someone ghastly from accounts, then you are going to have to spend valuable unsociable time being sociable and talking to them. Makes me feel positively stressed at the thought.

It's not even that rare. In a survey, eight out of ten of the people claimed to have done so. Most of us will pretend not to have noticed one another until the night before we leave... then suddenly do a double take and pretend to be *so* disappointed that we hadn't been able to spend much more holiday time together.

THE WEATHER

Thing is the one thing above all else which will determine whether your holiday works or not is the weather, and that's the one thing that you have absolutely no control over at all. Even if you're Elton John, going down to reception and complaining that it's too windy or too rainy will do absolutely nothing at all to change it. Might make you feel better, though.

Face it, with many package-deal destinations, you're only there for the sun and sand and sea, and if the sun doesn't come out the resort can be very unappealing. Without the sun, some of these resorts are about as attractive as Swindon.

> *I remember sort of lighting a fire and sort of having to put my fake tan on to a roaring fire, and I thought, This is a bad, bad holiday.*
>
> Jenny Eclair

> *When you go on holiday, of course, there are the days when it rains and that is the opportunity to pass the misery that you suffered as a child on to the next generation, so it's time to*

look at the inside of churches. Cos what could be more inter-
esting to a child than some stained glass that's made by quite
a famous stained-glass artist, children?

John O'Farrell

They all go, 'Oh, it was really sunny last week, oh, the weath-
er forecast is good for next week and you feel like saying, 'Yes,
well, I'm not here next week, am I, and I wasn't here last week.
I am here this week.'

Linda Robson

People are always saying to me, because they think I have
something to do with the weather, I am the rain goddess. They
always say to me, 'The farmers will be so grateful,' and I say,
'Fuck the farmers' and they say to me, 'I am so thrilled for the
garden.' I don't care about the garden. I am very selfish: I want
to know about me, and when I am going to get a suntan, but
it doesn't happen.

Nina Myskow

GOING HOME

When the holiday starts to draw to a close, as draw to a close it
must, the truth is that grumpy people are sorryish, but there is

A Russian woman sued weather forecasters for ruining her
holiday with incorrect predictions. She told the court that she
had been promised temperatures of 28 degrees and constant
sunshine during her weekend camping trip, but instead got
wet through when it did nothing but pour down with rain the
entire time.

a little voice, which is the thought that getting back into your own bed is starting to appeal – even getting back into the normal routine. And if holidays have any purpose, this surely is it. It doesn't half make you appreciate home.

> *The only purpose a holiday actually serves is to make me appreciate my house a little bit more. That's really ... yes, I'll have spent £2,000 or £3,000 taking us all away to come back to feel that. Oh, of course it makes you feel better about the area, because I haven't been broken in to, so then I decide I live in a completely crime-free zone.*

> *Arabella Weir*

And then just to round things off nicely on the grumpy front, you realise just how much the holiday cost you. Cosy as it is to realise that you appreciate home more than ever, it is a horribly costly lesson to learn.

Counting the cost

The British spend a staggering 6 billion on their holidays each year – not on posh hotels or long-haul flights, but on bits and pieces before we go. The average holiday will cost £490, but in reality we are more likely to spend £1,154 by the time we've stocked up with new gear and things we need to go away. And that's just for one holiday. The majority of us are likely to go on two breaks per year, according to one poll, and one in twenty of us manage to get away up to five times a year.

Over a quarter of families believe they spend more money on buying stuff in preparation for their holiday than on the holiday itself. The survey showed that the Scottish are the biggest pre-holiday spenders, compared to people in East

Anglia, who are the most frugal. A shopping list for the average Brit will contain the following:

- New clothes £88
- Toiletries £29
- Pre-holiday pampering £26
- Books and magazines £12
- Batteries, films, tapes £13
- New gadgets £40
- Sweets £5
- Beach kit £26
- Travel insurance £26
- Airport presents £32
- Spending money £314

Even when the holiday is over, half of us buy something in the airport before the flight, spending on average £32.

Recent research showed a third of people said that they do not expect to pay for their holiday within one statement, and one in six said that it would take them between four and six months to pay the bill. One in 50 said that they would still be paying for their holiday when they are packing their bags to go away the following summer.

HOLIDAYS IN RETROSPECT

Holidays are in reality a bit like parties: you have a short memory when it comes to them. Like parties, as you get older, holidays are really not the carefree, fun-filled time you thought they used to be, but you manage somehow to delete the bad bits. In retrospect it seems that the holiday really was worth all

Holidays are bad for health

On top of making you overdrawn, a holiday sometimes even makes you ill, apparently.

A growing number of people are having to take time off work when they get back from their holidays to recover from accidents or illness. A survey of 500 adults showed that some have taken at least two weeks off after falling ill or having an accident during a break.

the money and time spent on it and the more time that's elapsed, the better the holiday seems and the more likely you are to forget the bits you hated. That hideous holiday cruising round Norway feeling seasick all the way suddenly becomes a jolly jape when you dine out and recount the experience ten years later...

So we're going to carry on going on holiday – even us grumpies.

On the other hand, you could come to your senses and not go on holiday at all.

I get excited about holidays, even if, like, you know that a holiday's just sort of watching GMTV for a morning sick rather than going to work. Even if it's just that, it's just the absence of things you've got to do, isn't it? That's what's lovely about them.

Stuart Maconie

Holidays can never possibly live up to your expectations because you want everything from a holiday. So of course they disappoint. It is never hot enough, you're never thin enough, the meals are always too expensive, you never had enough ice cream and you come back fatter.

Nina Myskow

Holidays aren't compulsory, after all. You could stop trying to have the trip of a lifetime, give up on the exhausting process of trying to have the time of your life, and just stay put. Shut the front door, take the phone off the hook, and cosy up in your own comfort zone – at home.